IMAGES
of Rail

Northern Central Railway

Calvert Station was the southern terminus of the Northern Central Railway (NCR) in Baltimore, Maryland. One of the NCR's predecessor companies, the Baltimore & Susquehanna Railroad (B&S), opened its first station on July 4, 1831, at the corner of North and Eager Streets. B&S officials named the new structure Belvidere Depot after the Belvidere estate of John Eager Howard, a former governor of Maryland and an early advocate of local railroads. As business expanded and railroad technology advanced, B&S Railroad leaders realized they needed a bigger facility to handle the influx of business. Unforeseen circumstances soon led to an opportunity. In 1847, a Roman-style amphitheater at the corner of Calvert and Franklin Streets burned to the ground. The disaster allowed the railroad to purchase the desirable property in the center of Baltimore City close to city hall. This was an excellent location for the B&S Railroad to expand its business while providing goods and services to city residents. After the sale of the property was finalized, the railroad quickly hired one of Baltimore's most prestigious architectural firms, Niernsee & Neilson, to design and supervise the construction of Calvert Station. The railroad opened the nearly completed building to the general public on June 3, 1850. At that time, the impressive Calvert Station was the largest railroad terminal in the United States. (Courtesy Robert L. Williams Collection.)

On the Cover: The Northern Central Railway Calvert Station is shown here in 1890. The station was located near the center of Baltimore City, which allowed railroad patrons to access many of the amenities that the city has to offer. Note the cable streetcars running in front of the station; this was one of three cable car routes established in Baltimore City at that time to conveniently transport riders throughout the city. (Courtesy Robert L. Williams Collection.)

IMAGES
of Rail

NORTHERN CENTRAL RAILWAY

Robert L. Williams

ARCADIA
PUBLISHING

ISBN 978-1-4671-0344-2

Published by Arcadia Publishing
Charleston, South Carolina

Printed in the United States of America

Library of Congress Control Number: 2018963470

For all general information, please contact Arcadia Publishing:
Telephone 843-853-2070
Fax 843-853-0044
E-mail sales@arcadiapublishing.com
For customer service and orders:
Toll-Free 1-888-313-2665

Visit us on the Internet at www.arcadiapublishing.com

This book is dedicated to my beloved son Kyle James Williams and my good friends Ken Myers and Bob Ketenheim

Contents

ACKNOWLEDGMENTS

I would like to take this opportunity to share a very special thank you to Bob Ketenheim, for without Bob's experience, knowledge, and patience, this book would not have been possible.

All of the photographs within this publication are from the author's Robert L. Williams Collection. Through the years, many rail historians and railfans have donated photographs to increase my collection. I would like to take this opportunity to thank the following individuals for their contributions, which made this publication possible: Barry Arnold, Robert E. Base, Allen Brougham, C.B. Chaney, Milton A. Davis, Rudy Fisher, Ivan E. Frantz Jr., Martin Gemmill, Bob Gunnarsson, Gregory Halpin, Herbert H. Harwood Jr., Bud Hatfield, W.R. Hicks, E.H. Hinrichsman Jr., Robert W. Janssen, Roland R. Klages, Betty J. Lewis, Bill Lewis, Charles Lewis, Charles T. Mahan, John McGrain, Francis Chenoweth Miller, Frank Tyre Miller, Kenny Myers, George F. Nixon, Warren E. Olt, George Pitz, George L. Platz, Fred Rasmussen, C. Stewart Rhine, Bruce D. Sellman, F.G. Tatnall Jr., Martin Van Horn, Russell L. Wilcox, J.W. Wolf, and Frank A. Wrabel.

A special thank-you goes to Scott L. Mingus Sr., an award-winning Civil War historian and author of 24 books, for his review and editing of this publication. Special thanks also go to the following organizations for their contributions: Maryland Historical Society; Maryland Archives; Baltimore County Historical Society; Baltimore County Public Library; *Baltimore News American*; *Baltimore Sun*; National Archives; Pennsylvania Railroad Museum in Harrisburg, Pennsylvania; New Freedom Public Library; and York County History Center.

INTRODUCTION

Come take a sentimental journey along a true north–south railroad that ran through the heart of Maryland and Pennsylvania for more than 14 decades, allowing goods and services to flow through the mighty ports of Baltimore and Philadelphia. This railroad's humble beginnings started in Baltimore in 1827 with its predecessor, the Baltimore & Susquehanna Railroad, and by 1854, its constituent lines had pushed northward into the Keystone State almost 100 miles (to Sunbury).

After the consolidation of six separate railroads in 1854, the Northern Central Railway (NCR) was born. The NCR's strategic location led to economic success for Baltimore and Philadelphia. During the Civil War, the NCR proved to be a mighty economic powerhouse and played a key role in the outcome of the war. It expanded by leasing and later acquiring another railroad that ran north to Elmira, New York, where the Union army established a major prisoner-of-war camp. After the war, the NCR's popularity and economic growth continued as new railroads, which were building east–west routes, had to either connect to the NCR or pass over it. Due to the successful management of the NCR, the Pennsylvania Railroad, being the majority stockholder, moved to obtain complete control of the NCR by leasing it. The proposal was brought to the stockholders of the NCR, and they unanimously voted to give the Pennsylvania Railroad complete control of the railroad through the lease dated July 29, 1914.

However, the introduction of the automobile in 1913 abruptly halted the NCR's steady growth. As the automobile and then the cargo truck continued to gain popularity among the general public, the NCR experienced a decline in passenger and freight services. With this decline, the NCR, for economic reasons, abandoned all local passenger trains and consolidated freight movements by 1965. The Pennsylvania Railroad started abandoning sections of the line in 1956. Hurricane Agnes destroyed many sections of track and bridges along the route from Baltimore to Sunbury in 1972, accelerating the death of the former NCR.

Although the NCR's glory years have faded into history, future generations will be able to recall the railroad's past achievements due to many sections of its abandoned right-of-way being revitalized and turned into nature and bicycle paths.

Pictured is a 1930s view of Calvert Station's ticket office. Note the gaslight fixture at the top of the image. Calvert Station was the first railroad facility in the United States to use natural gas to provide illumination for the depot's headhouse and train shed.

One

The Beginning

On July 24, 1827, a group of progressive and enthusiastic Baltimore businessmen appointed by the York Haven Company and several toll road operators from Pennsylvania met on a hot summer day in a small office facing Pratt Street in downtown Baltimore City. They were there to discuss the possibility of building a railroad from the port of Baltimore to York Haven, located 11 miles north of York, Pennsylvania. Several meetings ensued, and on August 15, the Baltimore businessmen met with local officials in York Haven to report that the construction of such a railroad was feasible. There were no insurmountable obstacles, they announced, based on a recent report from civil engineers William F. Small and J.G. Swift.

The business leaders then returned to Baltimore and reported to the Maryland State Legislature that all concerned parties were in favor of the construction of said railroad. With the full support of the legislature, a charter was granted on February 13, 1828. The Baltimore & Susquehanna Railway Company held its first meeting on May 5 of that year, with company officials electing George Winchester as the first president of the newly formed entity.

On August 8, 1829, the 100th anniversary of the incorporation of Baltimore City, the Baltimore & Susquehanna formally laid its cornerstone. Construction began 10 days later.

The passenger platforms and entrance to the train shed in the back of Calvert Station are shown above. The shed was 315 feet long and 112 feet wide. When completed, it contained two passenger tracks and three freight tracks. After 1860, when new facilities (including Freight Shed A) were constructed north of the station and at Bolton Yards, all the tracks within the train shed were designated as passenger tracks. The head wall to the train shed and entrance was built entirely of brick, with a thick layer of plaster covering the brick to match the facade of the main station. The train shed used the queen-rod principle for the Howe trusses that supported the roof. At the time, it was the largest train shed in the United States. Steam engines were not permitted inside the train shed. Because of the steep grade between Bolton Station and Calvert Station, during the 1850s, 1860s, and 1870s, engines would be cut off, allowing passenger trains to coast from Bolton Station and switch into the train shed. After 1873, the engines of passenger trains headed toward Calvert Station were cut off at the Charles Street Depot. Another engine was placed at the back end of the passenger train to shove it to Calvert Station and then into the train shed; in those cases, the locomotives stayed outside the shed.

This is Calvert Station as it appeared in 1947. On May 14, 1932, the railroad transferred all freight activity to President Street Station. The only other train to enter and leave the station was the Parkton Local, which traveled from Calvert Station to Parkton, Maryland, and back after the completion of the Baltimore & Potomac Railroad Tunnel, the Charles Street Depot, and Union Tunnel in 1873. This gave passengers a direct route from Washington, DC, to New York City without having to change trains or experience delays while engines were switched. As a result, the importance of Calvert Station as a central hub for passenger service declined to the point where the railroad abandoned the complex and sold it to the Sun Papers in 1947. By 1948, Calvert Station's prominence among the great architectural wonders in Baltimore came to an abrupt end when it was demolished to make way for the new facilities of the *Baltimore Sun*.

The NCR's general office building is pictured in the 1890s. As business continued to flourish, the facilities at Calvert Station became inadequate. The railroad needed additional space, so in 1876, the NCR erected this 80-by-50-foot general office building at the corner of Calvert and Centre Streets. The redbrick structure opened on March 1 of that year.

The Parkton Local is shown leaving Calvert Station and passing under the elevated Gilford Avenue trolley line. Railroad employees and trolley men often struggled with each other. At times, a train passing under the elevated trolley tracks would wait until a trolley car would come along. When the trolley was directly above the train's locomotive, the engineer would blow smoke out of the smokestack directly into the trolley car. After trolley men became wise to this antic, they began carrying buckets of bolts with them. Once they were in position directly over the locomotive, the trolley men would drop a handful of bolts through the elevated tracks into the engine's smokestack, causing loud noises.

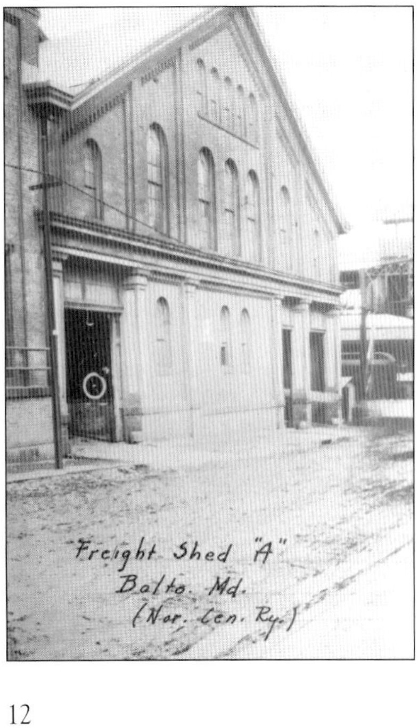

This is Freight Shed A as it appeared in 1916. With the advent of Civil War in the spring of 1861, the NCR became a vital conduit for moving military supplies and Union troops from the north into Washington, DC. With this increase in activity, Calvert Station soon proved inadequate to handle the large volume of inbound and outbound freight. On April 1, 1865, the NCR opened Freight Shed A, a massive 383-by-150-foot brick warehouse on the west side of Gilford Avenue just north of Calvert Station. The building stood the test of time before the Penn Central Railroad finally abandoned it in the 20th century. The railroad eventually sold the structure to the Downtown Athletic Club, which has preserved it. The striking building is a reminder to passing motorists on the Jones Falls Expressway of the railroad's once-strong presence in Baltimore.

The interior of Freight Shed A is pictured in the 1960s. From 1948 to 1959, Freight Shed A served as the station for the Parkton Local. Affectionately nicknamed "Calvert Station" in honor of the facility that was demolished in 1948, it had two tracks (with a platform in the middle of the two tracks), a small waiting room, and a ticket office.

The Parkton Local is shown leaving Freight Shed A on a fine day in May 1959. It made several station stops on its way north to Parkton.

NCR grain elevator No. 2 was located on the northwest corner of Monument and Beuren Streets. It opened on August 20, 1891, and expanded the railroad's capacity to take on additional grain business that the existing elevator in Canton could not handle.

In the early 1830s, Baltimore officials—worried that steam engines might cause fires at nearby wooden structures—passed an ordinance forbidding steam engines from operating under power within city limits. For decades thereafter, various railroads, including the NCR, used teams of powerful draft horses to pull heavily laden freight cars through the streets. The use of horsepower continued until 1916, when the railroad introduced a battery-operated electric tractor to pull freight cars within the city.

A Pennsylvania Railroad electric tractor is pictured here in 1940. Widely known as the "Rubber Tire Switcher," the battery-powered tractor pulled and shifted freight cars at the Madison Street freight yard located near the Baltimore City Jail.

This 1940s view looks south from the Eager Street overhead bridge and shows the Gilford Avenue elevated trolley tracks (at right) and the Madison Street freight yard leading to Freight Sheds E and F (center). Between the 1870s and 1900s, the Northern Central Railway built five more freight sheds on the east side—and one on the west side—of Gilford Avenue.

This is a 1929 view of the turntable at North Street (later renamed Gilford Avenue). Built in 1891 along with a 12-stall brick engine house, the turntable had a radius of 69 by 15 feet. It serviced all the trains coming off the Northern Central Railway from Calvert Station. On December 31, 1900, the railroad converted the engine house to a storage and power house. The building caught fire in 1913 and was gutted; it was soon demolished.

This 1978 view looking north shows the Union Junction interlocking and signal tower with the Gilford Avenue overhead bridge in the background. The tower received its name after the Union Railroad, a subsidiary of the NCR, connected its tracks to the NCR's main line in Baltimore near the Charles Street Depot (later renamed Union Station). This created a junction point between the two railroads, yielding a direct route to Philadelphia via the Philadelphia, Wilmington & Baltimore Railroad north of Baltimore. The tower, built in 1911, had a telegraph call sign of "CS."

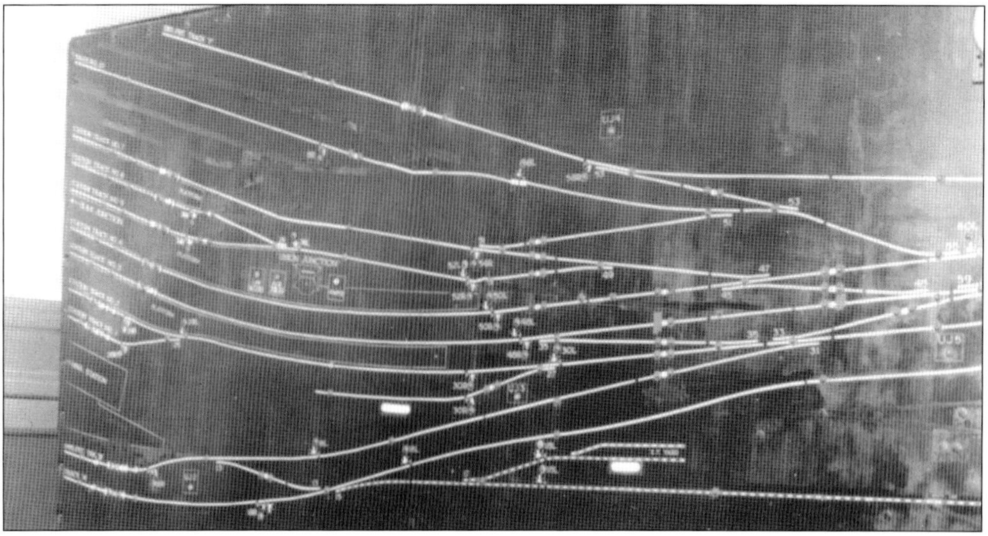

The Union Switch and Signal Company of Swissvale, Pennsylvania, installed Union Junction's interlocking model board in 1911. It is shown here in 1978. The model board assisted the lever man or the operator in visualizing which switches to engage and what route to establish for either the entrance or exit of the interlocking train. After the route was established, the model board would show the operator which signals to engage to let the engineer of the train know that the route had been established. The train could then proceed according to the signal indications. Indication lights on the model board allowed the operator to know that a train was occupying a particular track. Lights also conveyed information on the direction of traffic, which signals were engaged, and the movement of the train through the interlocking.

This is a 1978 view of Union Junction's electropneumatic machine that the Union Switch and Signal Company also installed in 1911. This machine consisted of 95 levers and allowed the operator to engage the lever from inside the tower. In response, the corresponding switch or signal in the interlocking would move. In all, 26 levers controlled the signals, 39 handled the switches, and 16 managed the traffic. There were 14 spare levers.

Robert Williams, the last daylight operator at the Union Junction interlocking and signal tower, posed for the camera in the early morning on May 20, 1987, for the last time, knowing that the doors of the old tower would be closed that night and the lights turned out forever. At 1:41 a.m. on May 21, Jeff Kirchner, the midnight operator, watched as Amtrak personnel disconnected all of the signals and switches that the tower controlled. From then on, control came from the Baltimore & Potomac (B&P) Junction interlocking and signal tower located on the south end of Penn Station in Baltimore City.

A northbound passenger train is shown leaving Penn Station and passing the Union Junction interlocking and signal tower in 1947. Famed industrial designer Raymond Loewy designed the GG1 electric locomotive that is shown pulling a passenger train. The locomotive was placed into service in 1934.

This is one of three Union Stations built by the railroad near the Charles Street overhead bridge. The NCR constructed the first station, known as the Charles Street Depot. That depot was sandwiched between the Baltimore & Potomac Railroad tunnel to the south and the Union Railroad tunnel to the north. The construction of these two tunnels in 1873 created a direct route from Washington, DC, to Philadelphia and New York. The small wooden-frame structure had a two-track train shed. All of the tracks were aligned toward Calvert Station, because the railroad never anticipated that the Charles Street Depot would draw much business. However, between 1873 and 1883, traffic grew at such an unexpected rate that the railroad had to consider building a more substantial structure.

This is an 1890 view of the second Union Station built by the NCR near the Charles Street overhead bridge. In 1885, the company, realizing that the first Union Station was not suited to handle the tremendous growth in business, replaced it with a large redbrick structure measuring 60 by 200 feet and a four-track train shed measuring 76 by 360 feet. The doors to the new building, also known as the Charles Street Depot, opened to the general public on April 1, 1886.

The main lobby of the second Union Station is shown here in 1890. The grand staircase led to a public restaurant and the railroad's office on the second level.

This 1898 view of the train shed looks north. Note the wide platforms, which allowed for easier loading and unloading of baggage and freight than the older shed.

This 1890s view shows a Baltimore & Potomac Railroad passenger train with engine No. 318 heading south out of the Charles Street Depot. Note the train shed in the background.

This 1910 photograph was taken during the construction of the third Union Station. At this point, freight and passenger traffic had grown to the point where the second Union Station could no longer service these needs. Hence, a larger facility was planned. At right is the temporary station that served the railroad until the main station was completed.

Penn Station (pictured above in 1940) was completed on August 1, 1911, at a cost of $700,000. Kenneth M. Murchison of New York City designed it. The name was later changed to Union Station because of the six separate railroads that converged at the station and utilized its facilities. The station underwent a face-lift in the 1930s to improve operations. Around that time, workers constructed a second Union Tunnel to relieve congestion as well as adding overhead catenary wires to permit electric engines to run in and out of the station. This facilitated the separation of local trains from through trains that were heading north to New York City or south to Washington, DC. Below is a 1912 view of the main waiting room at Union Station. The room measured 65 feet wide by 95 feet long and had a 35-foot-high ceiling decorated with ornamental stained glass, which permitted natural light to filter through. During World War II, the stained-glass panels were painted black to prevent the show-through of interior lighting. This was done in case an enemy decided to attack Baltimore; hostile pilots would not be able to locate the station from the air.

The Union Station baseball team is pictured in 1913. The Northern Central/Pennsylvania Railroad encouraged and promoted athletic events among employees and their families. Corporate leaders believed that a healthy employee was productive and safe while executing his or her duties.

The Penn Station platforms and tracks are pictured here in 1940.

A passenger train proceeds south from Union Station in 1912. Note the 31,000-gallon wooden water tank (to the left of the tracks), which allowed steam engines to take on water before leaving the station.

The Baltimore & Potomac interlocking just south of Union Station is shown here in 1912. Station tracks one through four were aligned toward the Baltimore & Potomac Tunnel, while tracks five through eight were aligned toward the NCR's main line. Switches and crossovers permitted trains to move from one track to another, allowing them to head south to Washington, DC, or north to Harrisburg, Pennsylvania. Northbound trains out of Washington would be switched through the interlocking to the designated track so they could proceed north to New York City.

This 1912 view of the B&P Junction interlocking and signal tower looks south with the North Avenue overhead bridge in the background. The tower received its name when the Baltimore & Potomac Railroad connected with the main line of the NCR in Baltimore City near the Charles Street Depot (later renamed Union Station). This connection created a direct route from Washington, DC, to Baltimore. The tower, completed in 1911, had the telegraph call letters "GU."

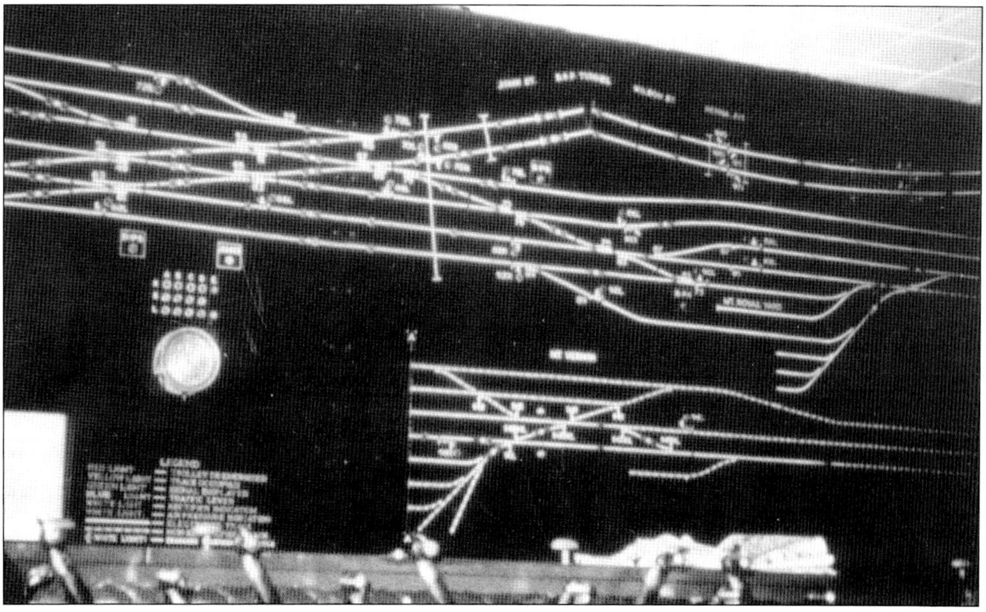

This B&P Junction interlocking model board was installed in 1911 by the Union Switch and Signal Company; it is pictured here in 1953. The company also installed the electropneumatic machine. This machine consisted of 107 levers that allowed the operator to engage the lever from inside the tower, and either the switch or signal would respond in the interlocking outside the tower. The machine had 32 levers for signals, 49 levers for switches, 14 traffic levers, and 12 spare levers.

The North Avenue (originally named Boundary Street) overhead bridge was built in 1895. This 1910 view shows the B&P Tunnel on the left. The tunnel was built in 1872 by the Baltimore & Potomac Railroad with financial backing from the Pennsylvania Railroad. A cut-and-cover method was used to construct the tunnel that opened a direct route to Washington, DC.

The entrance to Bolton Station is shown in 1916. The history of this station goes back to 1832, when it was built and operated as the first major terminal for the Baltimore & Susquehanna Railroad. By 1870, Baltimore officials needed the property housing Bolton Station to expand city streets to accommodate steady growth in the area. By then, Mount Royal Avenue, Oliver Street, Bolton Street, and Maryland Avenue bounded the Bolton Station facilities. In exchange for the railroad's cooperation, the City of Baltimore deeded over a parcel north of Boundary Street (later renamed North Avenue) along the NCR's main line.

Bolton Station is pictured here in 1910. The station was a frame structure measuring 33 by 329 feet. Built in 1872, it housed a small ticket/freight office and a large freight warehouse. The railroad demolished the structure in the 1950s as business declined.

The NCR's Bolton Freight Yard consisted of 12 coal trestles, 10 storage tracks, and 1 large crane. The entrance to the freight yard was controlled by the Baltimore & Ohio Railroad's "NA" interlocking and signal tower. The B&O tracks crossed the Bolton Yard's tracks at grade. The freight yard is shown here in the 1920s.

The entrance to the Mount Vernon Shops and Freight Yard is pictured above in 1916. At right are the smokestack and fan house for the B&P Tunnel. Steam engines passing through the tunnel generated tremendous clouds of thick smoke; the high-powered fan drew the smoke out of the tunnel and exhausted it into the air. The Mount Vernon Shops and Freight Yard are shown below in 1916. Built in the 1870s, the facility consisted of a large brick roundhouse with a diameter of 289 feet that housed the steam engines, a paint shop, blacksmith shop, transfer table, machine shop, powerhouse, car shop, mill, stock room, lumber shed, seven storage tracks, northbound–southbound freight track, and the two main line tracks of the NCR.

The Mount Vernon Produce Terminal was completed in 1930. The Pennsylvania Railroad also operated large repair facilities in Orangeville, Maryland; Enola, Pennsylvania; and Altoona, Pennsylvania. PRR officials believed that the repair facilities at Mount Vernon no longer served a need, especially because the roundhouse had burned down in 1911. Therefore, the railroad decided that since the fresh produce market was experiencing tremendous growth, it would build a new facility. The ensuing produce terminal consisted of a large brick warehouse and 10 tracks with concrete platforms to handle the loading and unloading of fresh produce.

A southbound freight train is shown passing the KN interlocking and signal tower. This tower, built in 1908, controlled the entrance and exit of trains on the NCR's main line as well as the repair facilities at Mount Vernon. The Pennsylvania Railroad issued General Order 1611 abandoning KN on March 10, 1933, because of the installation of an automatic position light signal system. At right are the buildings of Mount Vernon Mills.

A northbound double-header freight train is shown pushing up the grade and passing by Meadow Mills in 1901.

This photograph offers a general view of the main line of the NCR. At right is the White Hall Mill, which dated to 1789.

An 1890s scene at Woodberry, Maryland, is pictured above near the Union Avenue grade crossing. At far left is the general store that once held a ticket office for the NCR. Just to the right of it is the Parks Mill.

Woodberry Station, pictured in 1965, was a 20-by-46-foot combination freight and passenger station built in 1877. The railroad demolished it in the 1970s.

The Frank G. Schenuit Rubber Company, shown above in 1940, purchased the old Parks Mill and renovated it as business expanded. During World War II, Schenuit enjoyed a substantial increase in business after winning government contracts to produce airplane tires. After the war, demand declined to the point that in 1962, the company declared bankruptcy and went out of business.

The 42-by-42-foot frame Melvale passenger station was built in 1892. It housed the living quarters for the stationmaster, the ticket office, and waiting rooms for men and women. A separate freight station was built and was located on the east side of the mainline tracks and the north side of Melvale Avenue (later renamed Cold Spring Avenue).

The passenger train station at Melvale, Maryland, is pictured above on March 30, 1926. A southbound passenger train was passing the station when pieces of ash and cinder reportedly flew out of the engine's smokestack and landed on the roof of the station, igniting it within minutes. The quick-thinking station agent managed to get word to the Mount Washington Fire Department, which rapidly responded and dispatched equipment to the scene to extinguish the blaze. In the 1959 image below, the Pennsylvania Railroad's E7A diesel locomotive No. 5768 and its train are heading south toward Melvale. Note the Baltimore Gas & Electric Company's natural gas storage tank in the background; it was later demolished to make way for a parking lot for the Mass Transit Administration Light Rail station at Cold Spring.

Clyburn Station is pictured here in 1916. The NCR had purchased a small section of Clyburn, the sprawling estate of prosperous Quaker businessman Jesse Tyson (1826–1906) along the Jones Falls north of Baltimore City. The railroad constructed a 14-by-22-foot frame depot in 1892. The NCR abandoned the short-lived Clyburn Station in 1919. Much of the remainder of Tyson's former property is now the Clyburn Arboretum.

This view of Mount Washington looks north up the NCR's main line in 1890. To the left, just south of the Mount Washington passenger station, is the Mount Washington Hotel. At one time, the hotel housed a small ticket office before the railroad station was built.

This iteration of the Mount Washington train station was a frame board-and-batten structure built with a touch of Gothic style. The original station or ticket office was located in the Mount Washington Hotel just south of the depot until 1859, when the railroad built a new station house. In 1873, sparks from a passing steam engine set that building on fire. In 1874, the railroad built a new station, which is shown here in 1916.

This train carrying the Duke and Duchess of Windsor is shown passing the Mount Washington Athletic Club (right) on October 11, 1941.

Relay (later renamed Hollins) got its name because of nearby stables located at the junction point where the Green Spring Branch and NCR met. From 1829 to 1852, horses were used to haul passenger trains from Baltimore to Owings Mills via the Green Spring Branch. At Relay, fresh horses were waiting for the passenger and freight cars to arrive so they could be changed out and proceed to Owings Mills. From 1832 to 1872, the ticket office was located in a tavern owned by private concerns. In 1876, the NCR purchased the land and built a new station (pictured).

The Buffalo Day Express is shown heading south to Baltimore in the autumn of 1959 while crossing the bridge at Lake Roland just north of Hollins.

This is the Brightside waiting shed as it appeared in 1882. Several large summer homes of prominent Baltimore businessmen were located in the area along with the railroad picnic grounds. During the summer months, the NCR dispatched special trains to bring people from the city to enjoy the cool country air at Brightside.

This is the Lake Station waiting shed as it appeared in 1940. In 1881, a proposal was forwarded to the NCR by the Baltimore & Delta Railway (B&D; later renamed the Maryland & Pennsylvania Railroad) to run a connection from the main line of the B&D in Towson, Maryland, and proceed eastward to the main line of the NCR at Lake Station. Because business was increasing in the area, the NCR built a station in anticipation of this connection being completed. The B&D Railway had started grading the right-of-way for the connection but stopped due to financial difficulties. In 1882, a fire destroyed the station. With renewed interest in a connection between Towson and Lake Station, the NCR built a new station in 1884, but financial difficulties again prevented the B&D Railway from pursuing the connection with the NCR.

In 1794, Nicholas Ruxton Moore, a Revolutionary War hero, purchased the land that would become Ruxton. Several prominent businessmen and their families settled in the area to get away from the heat and congestion of Baltimore City, and the development of an upper-middle-class community became a reality. In response to this development, the NCR erected a beautiful station in 1890 to reflect the charm and elegance of the community. Over time, as commuters began to prefer the automobile over the train, Ruxton Station lost its importance. In 1963, the station fell victim to the wrecking ball to make way for an apartment complex.

Elisa Potts, Ruxton Station's last agent, is shown posing with her grandson Tyre Miller on the station's platform. Potts was loved by all the commuters that used the Parkton Local—or the "Ruxton Rocket," as it was affectionately known by many who commuted to and from their homes to their jobs in Baltimore City. Potts raised chickens at the station. She was often seen chasing the chickens down the station platform to catch them when they got loose.

Frank Tyre Miller was a World War II veteran who gave 46 years of service to the Pennsylvania Railroad. Here, he is riding his horse and posing at the Ruxton Station platform in 1959. During World War II, Miller and his wife lived in the station after their marriage. They held their wedding reception at the station, then boarded a train at Ruxton and headed to Harrisburg, Pennsylvania, for their honeymoon.

The Pennsylvania Railroad's southbound Liberty Limited is shown passing under the Ruxton Road overhead bridge on its way to Washington, DC, via Baltimore. The Liberty Limited, one of three elite modern PRR trains, provided luxury to passengers traveling from Chicago to Washington.

Russell S. Mellinger Sr. was one of many beloved conductors on the Parkton Local (fondly referred to by some as the "Ruxton Rocket") who cared about commuters and would often get to know them on a first-name basis. Mellinger would go the extra mile to ensure the comfort and safety of commuters while always having a kind word for all. There were many times when Mellinger would see a need and help out without hesitation. Mellinger met his lovely bride, Loretta, while taking tickets on the Parkton Local. In this photograph, Mellinger is giving the "all-clear" hand signal to the engineer so the Parkton Local can proceed.

The northbound Liberty Limited is shown passing under the Ruxton Road overhead bridge as it headed out on the long journey to Chicago.

This is the Riderwood Station (originally known as Sherwood) as it appeared in 1917. Many outstanding citizens did not want their community name to be associated with the Sherwood Distillery located in Cockeysville, Maryland. They drafted a petition and submitted it to the Pennsylvania Railroad to change the station's name from Sherwood to Riderwood. On May 23, 1913, after the completion of the new passenger station, the railroad changed the name. The old Sherwood Station was placed on a flatbed train car and hauled to Sparks, Maryland, where it served as that community's local station for many years.

This a 1930 northward-looking view of the tracks and station at Riderwood. Note the Joppa Road overhead bridge, which the NCR rebuilt in 1902.

This 1957 image shows the Stebbins Anderson Coal, Lumber, and Hardware business located just north of Riderwood Station. The business was founded in 1867 as the Cochrane Lumber Company. As development continued to push northward along the NCR, so did the Cochrane Lumber Company, which conducted business in each of the communities to facilitate their growth. In 1911, the company was sold, and the name was changed to Stebbins and Anderson. The company celebrated its 150th anniversary in 2017, and as of the publication of this book in 2021, it is still providing goods and services to the communities.

The southbound Buffalo Day Express is shown passing the Riderwood passenger station in the spring of 1959.

Dr. John G. Morris, a Lutheran minister, founded and named the community of Lutherville, which was one of five planned communities in the United States at the time. It was laid out along the NCR in 1852. The first ornate waiting shed, erected in 1855, stood on the east side of the tracks. The second station, located west of the tracks, was built by John R. Cockey, Esq., in 1861. The station was occupied by Jacob D. Smith, who worked as a storekeeper and ticket agent for the railroad. In 1872, cinders bellowing out of the smokestack of the engine of a passing freight train landed on the roof of the station, which caught fire and burned to the ground. Three years later, Cockey built a third train station on the site. He operated the station and a small store inside it until 1885, when the station was sold to the railroad.

Dr. John G. Morris realized the inadequacy of the small store located in the Lutherville train station, so in 1885, he responded by building the Lutherville General Store just north of the depot to accommodate the growing community.

The Parkton Local sits in front of the Lutherville passenger waiting shed in 1959. The conductor and assistant conductor are waiting for all of the passengers to board the train before it proceeds north to Parkton.

The Timonium Race Track and Grandstands are pictured here in 1910. It has been suggested by historians that Sarah Buchanan, the owner of the Bellefield Estate, changed the name of the estate to Timonium after the death of her husband, Archibald Buchanan, in 1785.

The history of the one-mile Timonium Race Track and Grandstands dates back to 1819, when prominent landowners the Bosleys and the Talbotts built and maintained it. Horse races were conducted every year until 1832, when the Baltimore & Susquehanna Railroad laid its rails through the racetrack. The racetrack was relocated east of the railroad tracks, and horse racing has been conducted every year since. The Maryland State Fair has been held at the racetrack since 1879 and continues to be a major annual event.

Train No. 502, Baltimore to Harrisburg, powered by EP20 No. 5865, is shown heading north while passing over the Timonium grade crossing in 1955.

In 1913, the Pennsylvania Railroad erected the Timonium Station, shown above in 1916, to replace the first station that dated from 1875. The railroad razed it in 1960.

Crowds of Marylanders showed up in Timonium to greet the Duke and Duchess of Windsor on October 11, 1941. The Duke of Windsor (the former king of Great Britain) abdicated the British throne to marry a divorced American socialite named Wallis Warfield Simpson.

These passengers at Timonium are shown boarding the Baltimore–Harrisburg train heading south to Baltimore.

This southbound passenger train is shown heading to Baltimore in 1941.

This view looks south from the Padonia grade crossing in 1956. The passenger waiting shelter (at right) was rebuilt by the Pennsylvania Railroad in 1941 and razed in 1960.

The hamlet of Texas, Maryland, emerged as an Irish community after the completion of the Baltimore & Susquehanna Railroad in 1832. This allowed for an increase in limekiln and quarry activities in the area, creating more demand for skilled and unskilled labor. With the rapid expansion of the railroad, a high grade of finished limestone could be processed and moved via rail to almost any destination. The quarries near Texas provided some of the high-finished limestone used to complete the Washington Monument in Washington, DC. In 1836, the Texas passenger station was built from stones quarried in the area. The building served as a cultural center for the community until the late 1950s, when a fire destroyed it.

Tenement housing at Texas, Maryland, was built by the limekiln and quarry companies to house their laborers. The housing was close to the railroad to give workers easy access to the job site.

This group of young ladies posed in front of the Texas passenger station in 1950 before boarding the southbound Parkton Local to Baltimore so they could do some shopping.

The Cockeysville V interlocking and signal tower was rebuilt in 1879 near Beaver Dam Road inside the wye tracks. Children from a nearby schoolhouse posed with railroad officials in front of the tower in 1895.

A Cockeysville Local turns on the wye track in 1890. The wye track was installed in 1879 and removed in 1935, when the independent Cockeysville Local and Parkton Local were merged into one local that ran from Baltimore to Parkton and back.

This is a 1916 view of the Cockeysville passenger train station. Cockeysville was established and named after the Cockey family, who settled in the area in 1725. The first commercial building in the area was a hotel built by Joshua Frederick Cockey in 1810. His son Judge Joshua Frederick Cockey II built the first train station in 1836 out of stone quarried a short distance from the town. In the early 1860s, the station caught fire and burned down. The railroad proceeded to purchase land from the Cockey family in 1865 to build a new station (above).

This 1912 view looks southwest toward the Susquehanna Trail (later renamed York Road) where the turnpike crosses the mainline of the NCR at grade. The York Road turnpike was a major route between Baltimore City and York before the construction of Interstate 695 (Baltimore Beltway) and Interstate 83 (Jones Falls Expressway).

A 1926 northward view of the Northern Central Railway tracks in Cockeysville is shown here. The V interlocking and signal tower at left was moved from its original location to York Road Turnpike in 1905. This allowed the railroad to eliminate the grade-crossing watchmen by transferring their responsibilities to the tower operator. PRR General Order No. 1115, dated September 20, 1930, eliminated the V interlocking and signal tower due to the invention of automatic position light signals and graded crossing gates.

This southbound Parkton Local pictured in 1921 is headed by a K4s engine, No. 3361. The grand Cockeysville train station stood the test of time until 1972, when Hurricane Agnes destroyed many railroad bridges and tracks. Due to the astronomical cost of repairing the railroad, Penn Central decided to abandon the track from Cockeysville to the Maryland state line. The station was razed in 1974.

This northward view shows the Cockeysville freight station that was built in 1903 to alleviate the congestion at the York Road Turnpike. The original freight house was located just north of the train station with its siding. However, when it was time to shift and drop off freight cars, it became difficult due to the freight train blocking the York Road Turnpike. This, in turn, backed up traffic leaving and entering Baltimore City from the turnpike.

Two

BALTIMORE LIGHT RAIL

Construction of the first seven miles of track from Belvidere Station (on the northern side of Baltimore City) to or near the Bellona Gun Powder Company (farther north in rural Baltimore County) commenced on August 18, 1829, with several hundred hands working vigorously. After many hardships and obstacles during the construction process, those first seven miles of track opened for business on July 4, 1831, with much celebration. Horse-drawn passenger cars and freight cars provided goods and services up and down the line. As businesses continued to develop along the new railroad line, so did the need to provide a special train to transport the labor force for these businesses to and from Baltimore City. On May 27, 1860, the NCR responded to this need by designating several trains to run from Baltimore City to Cockeysville, and the Cockeysville Local was born.

The Baltimore & Susquehanna Railroad (which was consolidated in 1854 into the newly created Northern Central Railway) continued to push northward to York, Pennsylvania, and beyond, and the need to extend local service was imperative. The Parkton Local was implemented on November 29, 1861, to run from Baltimore to Parkton so that homeowners in communities that had developed along the railroad could commute to Baltimore City. The Cockeysville Local remained in service until 1935, when the Pennsylvania Railroad (then owners of the old NCR) believed it would be more economical to combine both services into one and retain the name Parkton Local.

Because of declining revenue and direct competition with automobiles, the Pennsylvania Railroad ended the Parkton Local service on June 27, 1959. In 1972, Hurricane Agnes destroyed much of the railroad line from Cockeysville north. Baltimore mayor William Donald Schaefer saw the value of reestablishing a commuter line through northern Baltimore County. Throughout his tenure as mayor, Schaefer petitioned the State of Maryland to construct such a network tying Anne Arundel County and northern Baltimore County together by using existing railroad lines. On May 2, 1988, Schaefer (by then the governor of Maryland) signed a bill to allow the construction of the Baltimore Light Rail. By using the existing NCR right-of-way from Baltimore City to Cockeysville, history repeated itself, and the Cockeysville Local was reborn.

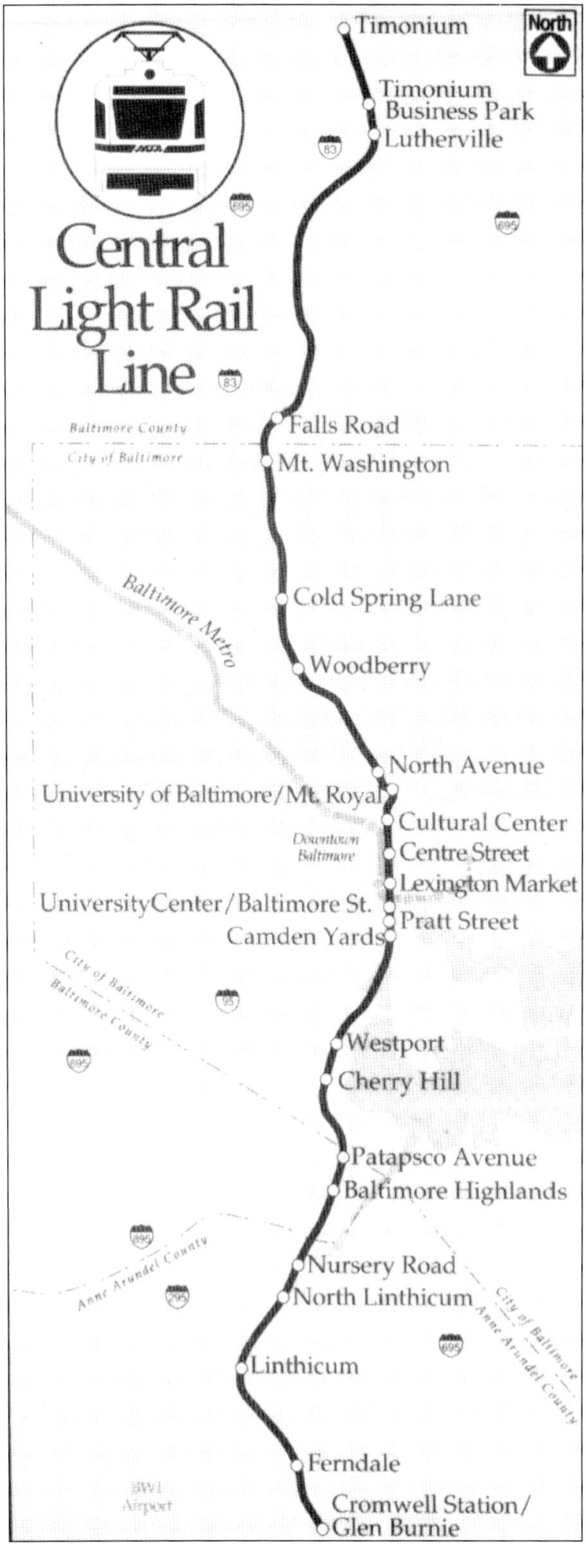

A map of the Baltimore Central Light Rail Line was officially released to the general public at its grand opening on May 22, 1992. The section from Timonium to Camden Yards was operational on April 3, 1992, and the section from Camden Yards to Cromwell Station opened on June 20, 1993. This completed the 22.5-mile light-rail system; it remained that length until November 1994, when the Maryland State Legislature approved and funded three extensions—Hunt Valley, Penn Station, and Baltimore/Washington International Thurgood Marshall Airport (BWI). On December 6, 1997, all three extensions were completed and opened to the traveling public.

The Baltimore Central Light (BCL) Rail Car and Repair Shops at Mount Vernon (located in Baltimore City) are shown above in June 2007. The Pennsylvania Railroad razed the original car and repair shops that the NCR built in 1872 and replaced them with a produce terminal and yard tracks in 1930. In 1988, the Maryland Transit Administration removed the PRR produce terminal to make way for the BCL shops.

A Baltimore Central Light Rail northbound train is shown passing under the Twenty-ninth Street overhead bridge built in 1938.

A Baltimore Central Light Rail train is shown heading south with the Wyman Park Drive overhead bridge in the background. At right is Wyman Park, part of the Baltimore City Park System; it dates to 1902, when Johns Hopkins University donated the land to establish a park.

A northbound CLR train is shown at Woodberry passing Meadow Mills (at right), which was built in 1877 by industrialist William E. Hopper. In 1960, the mill was sold to London Fog and remained in operation until 1988, when the company moved its operations to northwest Baltimore. The original NCR passenger station (at left) was built in 1877 and razed in the 1970s.

This southbound CLR train is passing the site of the original 1873 NCR passenger station at Mount Washington.

A northbound CLR train is shown crossing the railroad bridge over Lake Roland just north of Hollins. At Hollins, a branch line called the Green Spring Branch was completed on May 26, 1832, and made a connection at this location, forming a junction point. The Green Spring Branch Line served the western part of Baltimore County until December 18, 1959, when the railroad west of Rockland to Owings Mills was formally abandoned. In December 1961, the freight service formally ended when the branch line connection was removed from the main line.

A southbound CLR train is shown passing the original site of the NCR passenger station at Ruxton (left), which was built in 1890. It was torn down in 1963 to make way for an apartment complex.

The original Riderwood passenger station (pictured) was built by the Pennsylvania Railroad in 1913. It is currently still standing. The photograph was taken during the Light Rail Double Track Project that occurred between 2005 and 2006. A sound barrier was placed in front of the passenger station to reduce the noise of the passing light-rail trains.

This southbound CLR train is passing by the original Lutherville train station built by John G. Cockey in 1875 in Lutherville, Maryland. Cockey sold the station to the NCR in 1885. Due to declining ridership and competition with the automobile, the Pennsylvania Railroad sold the station to a private concern in 1960.

Here, a southbound CLR train is passing the original site where the NCR Timonium passenger station was located. The station was built in 1913 and torn down by the railroad in 1960.

A southbound CLR car No. 5005 and train are shown passing the original site where the Texas passenger station stood from 1836 until it caught on fire in the late 1950s.

The Baltimore & Susquehanna Railroad placed stone ties between 1830 and 1832. The stones were uncovered during the Light Rail Double Track Project that occurred between 2005 and 2006. They were preserved in place and are located near the Padonia Road overhead bridge. Iron strap rail (2½ inches by 9/16 inches) was nailed to longitudinal wooden stringers (6 inches by 6 inches by 6 feet) and then secured to marble stone blocks (15 inches by 16 inches by 16 inches) spaced every three feet apart and buried in the ground. The gauge between the iron strap rail was four feet, nine inches, and provided sufficient room for horses to pull either passenger or freight cars.

A northbound CLR car No. 5010 and its train are shown crossing the Warren Road grade crossing and proceeding northwest to the end of the line in Hunt Valley.

A southbound CLR car No. 5047 and train are getting ready to enter onto the original right-of-way of the NCR. At right is a spur track located on the original NCR right-of-way that ended in Cockeysville, Maryland. When the Hunt Valley extension was completed in 1997, it used the old Cockeysville industrial track that led to Hunt Valley.

Three

Northward to the State Line

The Baltimore & Susquehanna (B&S) Railroad's completion of its line from Baltimore City to Cockeysville, Maryland, on November 6, 1832, generated excitement, satisfaction, and goodwill among railroad officials who had hopes to continue the railroad's efforts to push northward to York Haven, Pennsylvania, and beyond. From 1829 through the early part of 1832, this excitement among B&S officials was constantly challenged by the Pennsylvania State Legislature, which repeatedly denied the railroad access into Pennsylvania.

In response to the Commonwealth of Pennsylvania denying the B&S direct access into York and beyond, an alternate route was developed that would move the railroad westward to Westminster, Maryland, and then have it proceed northeast, bypassing York and heading north to York Haven. The first eight miles of this alternate route were completed on May 26, 1832, and quickly became known as the Westminster Branch before construction was halted at Garrison Forest.

The Pennsylvania politicians finally compromised and granted a charter to the York & Maryland Line Railway (Y&ML) Company on March 14, 1832. This effectively gave the B&S what it had desired all long: a direct route heading north from Cockeysville, Maryland, to York and beyond to the Susquehanna River. Due to financial difficulties being experienced by the Y&ML, the B&S completed and operated the direct route from the Maryland state line to York starting on August 23, 1838.

The outward expansion of businesses and communities along the NCR from the 1840s through the early part of the 1860s created a need for a local commuter train to travel as far as Parkton, Maryland. The railroad responded by establishing the Parkton Local on November 29, 1861, to carry local commuters from Baltimore City to Parkton.

The NCR passenger station at Ashland, Maryland, shown here in 1916, was constructed in 1871. Ashland was named after the estate of Henry Clay, a prominent statesman and presidential candidate in the early 19th century. Ashland Iron Works was laid out and built on the east side of the tracks of the Baltimore & Susquehanna Railroad 16 miles north of Baltimore City in 1847. Just west of the railroad tracks, the company laid out and built the town of Ashland to accommodate those employed at the ironworks. Advancements in the processing of steel led to the demise of pig iron, causing the Ashland Iron Works to cease operations and close its doors forever in 1884.

The Jessop's Crossing (later renamed Ashland Road) overhead bridge, just north of Ashland, is pictured here in 1916. It was built in 1906 and razed in the 1970s.

This 1917 picture shows the NCR passenger station at Phoenix, Maryland, which was erected in 1890. The station consisted of men's and women's waiting rooms on either side of a central ticket office. The upper floor accommodated the living quarters for the stationmaster and his family. In 1946, the station caught fire and burned down.

This is a general view of Phoenix, Maryland, in 1890. Originally called Westerman's Mill, the settlement's name was changed to Phoenix in 1861 to reflect a name given by Thomas H. Fulton to a mill he built in 1847 and called the Phoenix Factory. In 1872, the mill changed hands when Robert Garrett and Joseph W. Jenkins purchased it and enlarged it. At the same time, the company that owned the mill laid out and built the town that surrounded it. At left is the covered bridge that was built in 1861. The CD interlocking and signal tower to the right of the bridge was rebuilt by the NCR in 1890 and abandoned by 1908.

This is a 1916 view of the NCR passenger station at Sparks, Maryland. This station was originally built in Sherwood (later renamed Riderwood), Maryland, in 1887 and was moved to Sparks by the railroad in 1913, when the Riderwood Station was completed. The original station is in the background at far right.

This is a picture of Sparks in 1946. Sparks, originally called Philopolis, was a small town east of the railroad tracks. In 1847, a post office was located in the area. It was not until 1911 that the US Post Office recognized and changed the name to Sparks to reflect the name of the family who had purchased and settled on a tract of land near the railroad. When the Sparks family contacted the NCR to install a switch and siding, it was commonly known as "Spark's Switch" by those who did business with the railroad. The general store was built in 1913, and the bank to the left of the store was constructed in 1916.

A Pennsylvania Railroad watch box located on the west side of the railroad tracks near the Sparks Road grade crossing is pictured here in 1946. A watchman would come out of the watch box and stop all traffic attempting to use the grade crossing so that oncoming trains could pass safely.

The Federal Engineering and Construction Company's stone quarry was located just south of Sparks. Here, a Northern Central Railway engine sits on the quarry siding in 1904.

This is a 1916 view of the first passenger station that was built in Glencoe, Maryland, in 1854. Between the 1860s and 1880s, the railroad embarked on an ambitious project to upgrade the road by building a second track and relining and straightening several curves. This station was converted into a home for the stationmaster in 1889 due to this ambitious project. The station has survived and was moved to White Hall, Maryland, for restoration.

The Glencoe combination passenger and freight station, pictured in 1917, was built on the west side of the tracks in 1889 and served as a passenger station and community center until 1957, when the Pennsylvania Railroad started downsizing by single tracking the railroad from York, Pennsylvania, to Baltimore City. The PRR converted the passenger side of the station into a signal and interlocking station in 1957 and used it until it was no longer needed due to the single tracking. The signal and interlocking station was closed by PRR General Order No. 805 on December 16, 1959. In April 1963, the shelter shed and remaining part of the passenger station were torn down.

This northbound NCR passenger train is getting ready to pass the GK interlocking and signal tower (right) and the watch box (left) in 1905 at Glencoe, Maryland.

This 1940 postcard shows the Glencoe Inn, which was built as a summer resort for Baltimore residents who wanted to escape the summer heat of the city. The prominent Mowell family, who owned the large tract of land in the 1870s, constructed the inn as well as a nearby lake with a boathouse.

The Glencoe post office is pictured in 1965 with the three women who ran the one-room office. *Ripley's Believe It or Not!* awarded this post office the dubious honor of being the smallest such facility in the United States. The boathouse that was located on the property of the Glencoe Inn was no longer in use, so it was moved to a site along Glencoe Road near the railroad tracks and converted to the post office. In the late 1960s, the post office was abandoned and moved to a spot along York Road. The small post office sat abandoned until the early 1980s, when officials from the Oakfield School for Girls moved the old building to the school's campus and restored it.

The NCR combination passenger and freight station at Corbett, Maryland, is shown above in 1916. The town was named after Isaac Corbett, who purchased a large tract of land near the railroad tracks and settled in the area. The town started showing significant growth when Robert Gwynn Merryman built a large sawmill and general store there in 1880. Responding to this continued growth, the railroad built the combined station in 1888. A. Harry became the first station agent at Corbett.

This 1890 view shows the general store at Corbett. It housed the local post office, general store, school classroom, and a church from 1890 to 1906. Note the school class posing in front of the general store. The building was later converted into a private residence and still stands; it can be seen from Corbett Road.

A northbound freight train is shown passing the passenger station and waiting shed at Corbett in 1960. After 1960, when the Pennsylvania Railroad completed its downsizing program by single tracking the railroad from Baltimore City to York, Pennsylvania, many of its structures fell prey to demolition. In April 1963, a contractor razed the passenger station and waiting shed.

In 1847, the Baltimore & Susquehanna Railroad (later known as the Northern Central Railway) built a small frame structure (above) that housed a ticket office and waiting room at Monkton, Maryland. As the community continued to experience growth, railroad officials recognized the need for a larger station, and in 1898, they built a combination passenger and freight station. Both of these photographs were taken in 1917. The first stationmaster to occupy the new station was Nicolas E. Miller. Below is a view of the stationmaster's house at Monkton that was built in or around 1880.

History repeats itself. During the Civil War, Union infantrymen were stationed along the NCR to protect the infrastructure and buildings against possible Confederate sabotage. During World War I, as fears of sabotage again arose, federal troops were once again stationed along the NCR. This 1916 photograph shows US soldiers encamped on Monkton Hill near the railroad tracks.

The Blue Mount, Maryland, station received its name from the nearby Blue Mount quarry, which produced large quantities of ballast stones for the railroad. The station, shown here in 1959, was rebuilt in 1940 and moved onto private property in 1960. Note the track crew installing a switch to the single track.

A northbound freight train derailed just south of Blue Mount on August 18, 1913, as captured by Pennsylvania Railroad photographer Jake W. Wolf.

White Hall, Maryland, derived its name from a large white house that was built close to the NCR tracks. At one time, this large white house was a station, post office, livery stable, and boardinghouse. The community started experiencing gradual growth after John Weise built a paper mill there in the early part of the 1800s. In 1883, the NCR built a combination passenger and freight station to accommodate the increase in growth and business. This photograph was taken in 1916.

The Pennsylvania Railroad's waiting shed at White Hall is shown above in 1950. Within the town limits, there were three railroad grade crossings along with the WH interlocking and signal tower that was rebuilt in 1897. It was removed from service by PRR General Order No. 309, dated May 18, 1929.

In this 1957 image taken at White Hall, Mary Smith is running to catch the southbound Parkton Local heading to Calvert Station in Baltimore City.

On June 6, 1934, a northbound Pennsylvania Railroad extra train derailed and plunged 30 feet into the Gunpowder River. The steam engine exploded, killing the engineer, the fireman, and the only passenger on the train, Margaret Frederick of Parkton, Maryland. Pictured at left, Frederick, who was 22 years old, was on her way home when it was said she waved to her father, who was a railroad watchman at White Hall, Maryland. Margaret's father waved back with a big smile on his face. Shortly after, the train derailed and fell into the Gunpowder River at Graystone, Maryland.

The grade crossing over the York Road Turnpike at Parkton, Maryland, is pictured above in 1920. Note the NCR watch box at right. A watchman was stationed at major grade crossings that were heavily traveled by the general public. The watchman would memorize the train schedule, and a couple of minutes before a train was due at the grade crossing, he would leave the watch box and step into the middle of the road while holding a stop sign. This would stop the public from attempting to cross the tracks, allowing the train to pass safely. Below, a northbound passenger train is shown entering Parkton in 1920. To the left is the combined Parkton Hotel, general store, and post office that was built in 1843. The hotel was built at the crossroads of two major transportation systems—the Baltimore & Susquehanna Railroad (later the NCR) and the Susquehanna Trail (later renamed York Road Turnpike). Each helped with the movement of goods and services and the growth of the community.

Parkton, Maryland, became a strategic stopping point on the railroad for freight trains heading north into Pennsylvania. These heavily laden trains had difficulties negotiating the 2.5 (to 3) percent grade between Parkton and New Freedom, Pennsylvania. The outward expansion and development of businesses and communities along the railroad compounded the problem. To meet the growing demand for services, the railroad completed additional passing tracks, a new passenger station, a turntable, an engine house, a water tank, and a small freight station by 1861. These facilities allowed helper engines to wait in Parkton to assist freight trains heading north, maintain equipment, and turn the new Parkton Local around so that it could head back to Baltimore City. By 1903, the small passenger station could not handle the volume of traffic, so the railroad built a new passenger station (pictured above in 1904). At right is the N interlocking and signal tower, which was rebuilt in 1899.

In 1907, the Pennsylvania Railroad built a reservoir on the hillside behind the Parkton passenger station to feed two large water tanks located just south of the station on the west side of the tracks. This 1920 photograph shows the town of Parkton beyond the reservoir.

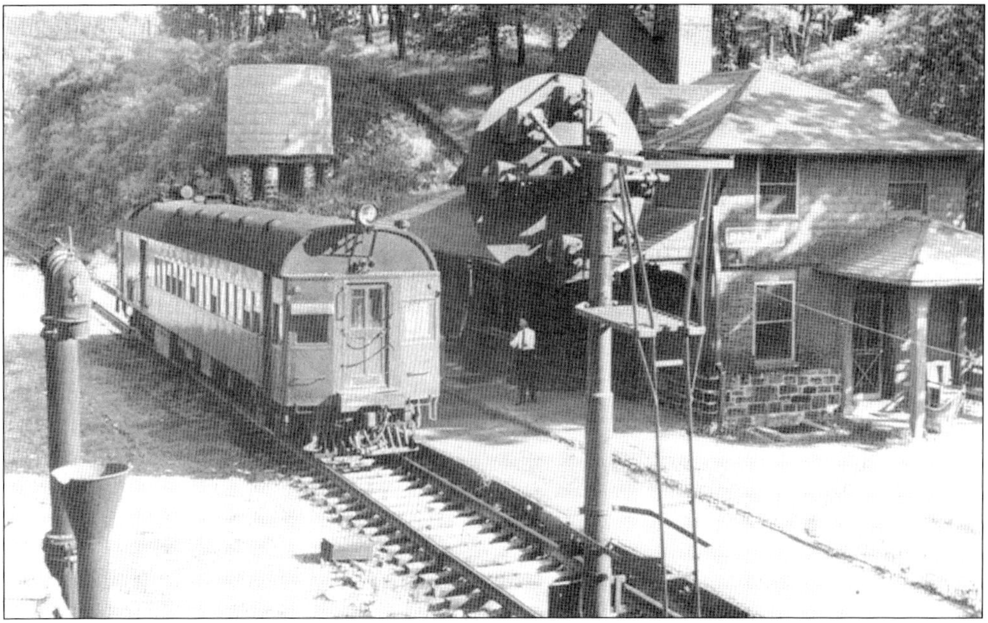

The Parkton Local's Car No. 4666 waits to proceed south to Baltimore City on June 4, 1959. This car, commonly referred to as a "Doodlebug," was built by the J.G. Brill Company in the 1930s as a gas and electric combination passenger and mail car. In 1940, as a result of a head-on collision in Ohio between a Doodlebug and a freight train, the Doodlebug's large gas tank exploded, killing all 47 passengers. The Pennsylvania Railroad immediately began retrofitting all of the Doodlebugs with diesel engines—a process the railroad had completed by 1942. The last run of a PRR Doodlebug took place in 1965.

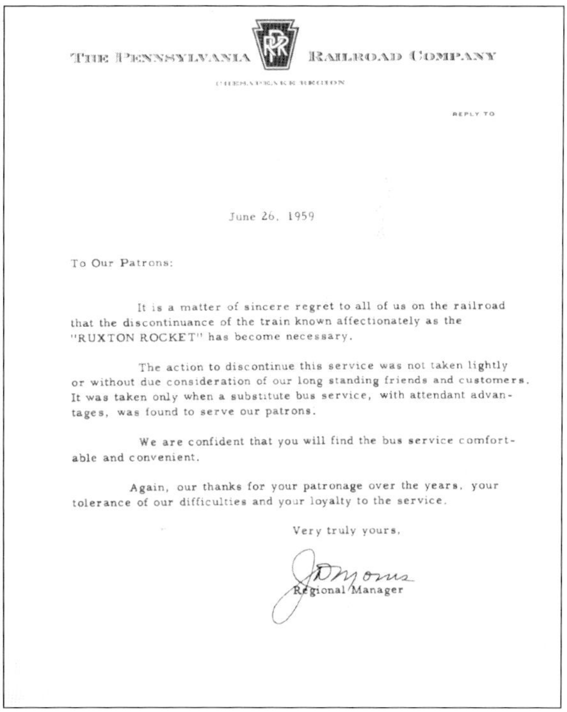

THE PENNSYLVANIA RAILROAD COMPANY

CHESAPEAKE REGION

REPLY TO

June 26, 1959

To Our Patrons:

It is a matter of sincere regret to all of us on the railroad that the discontinuance of the train known affectionately as the "RUXTON ROCKET" has become necessary.

The action to discontinue this service was not taken lightly or without due consideration of our long standing friends and customers. It was taken only when a substitute bus service, with attendant advantages, was found to serve our patrons.

We are confident that you will find the bus service comfortable and convenient.

Again, our thanks for your patronage over the years, your tolerance of our difficulties and your loyalty to the service.

Very truly yours,

J D Morris

Regional Manager

An official Pennsylvania Railroad notice informed customers that the Parkton Local (which was, as noted here, known affectionately as the "Ruxton Rocket") would be discontinued on or after June 26, 1959.

This father and son posed at the head end of Car No. 4666 after it pulled into the Parkton Station during its last northbound trip on June 27, 1959.

On June 27, 1959, the Parkton Local (train No. 527, car No. 4666) and its passengers waved farewell to the longtime service that had facilitated the growth and development of many communities along the Northern Central Railway for 98 years. It is gone but not forgotten.

Pennsylvania Railroad train No. 554, under the power of engine No. 5818, is shown passing the signal bridge and the Dairy Road grade crossing just north of Parkton before heading south to Baltimore City on September 3, 1949.

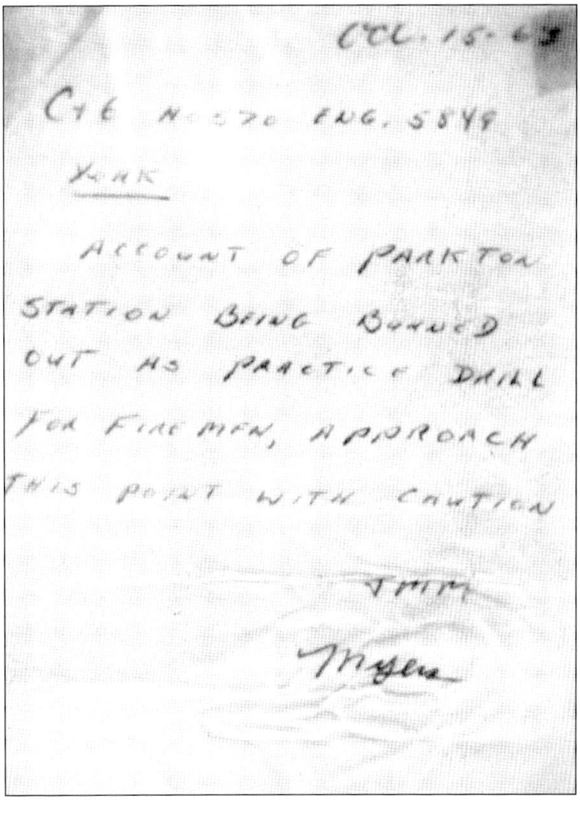
OCT. 15. 63

C+6 No. 570 ENG. 5849

YORK

ACCOUNT OF PARKTON STATION BEING BURNED OUT AS PRACTICE DRILL FOR FIREMEN, APPROACH THIS POINT WITH CAUTION

JMM

Myers

Conductor Russell S. Mellinger Sr., a beloved longtime employee of the Pennsylvania Railroad, received train orders (shown at right) in York, Pennsylvania, on October 15, 1963, to proceed south to Baltimore. He was asked to approach Parkton with caution because firemen were completing drills that involved setting the old passenger station on fire and then putting it out.

This image shows the AD interlocking and signal tower, which was located just south of the Bentley Springs passenger station on the west side of the NCR tracks near the Bentley Springs Road grade crossing. This 8-by-10-foot two-story frame structure was built in 1898 and controlled a set of grade crossing gates, two signals, and a crossover.

The NCR's combination passenger and freight station at Bentley Springs (pictured above) was built in 1859. This structure—which measured 24 feet, 6 inches, by 50 feet, 6 inches—was built of stone from quarries near Cockeysville. Located on the south end of the station were a small waiting room, ticket office, and stone-mantled fireplace with sand-finished walls. On the north end of the station was a large freight room. Note the boardinghouse located behind the station; it was built in the late 1890s to replace a hotel that had caught fire and burned down. The boardinghouse was razed in the early 1950s. Below is the Bentley Springs Hotel, which derived its name from Charles W. Bentley, who purchased a large tract of land and built the hotel with a grand marble courtyard near the NCR tracks in 1850. It became a favorite place for Baltimoreans to escape the summer heat. Adding to the success of the hotel, Bentley discovered cool spring water that would supposedly cure "all that ails you" and started bottling the water and shipping it south to Baltimore City.

Freeland, Maryland, derived its name from John Freeland, who purchased a portion of land that belonged to Isaac Morris. By 1837, the Baltimore & Susquehanna Railroad passed through the Freeland property on its way to York, Pennsylvania. The Freeland family seized on this opportunity and quickly built a small general store in 1850 that housed the post office and railroad ticket office. In 1857, the railroad built a 16,000-gallon water tank (left) to serve the steam engines. The RD interlocking and signal tower at left was rebuilt in 1899 and placed at the Freeland Road grade crossing. The tower controlled a crossover, two signals, and a pair of grade crossing gates. The tower was removed from service by PRR General Order No. 309, dated June 22, 1926. The combination passenger and freight station at right was completed in 1887; its doors closed to the general public in 1960. On January 8, 1962, at a cost of $1,200, the station was moved to the W. Doster Farm, where it still resides to this date.

The Freeland General Store is at left in this 1920 image. It is now a private residence. The Freeland Hotel (at right) was built around 1870 to serve those who wanted to flee the summer heat and congestion of Baltimore City.

Four

The York & Maryland Line Railroad

In October 1828, the newly formed Baltimore & Susquehanna (B&S) Railroad Company submitted a request to the Pennsylvania State Legislature for permission to build a railroad from the Pennsylvania/Maryland state line to York Haven, Pennsylvania, while passing through the bustling borough of York. After a heated debate among the legislators in 1829, a sectional faction from Philadelphia and vicinity prevailed, and the assembly denied the request for two reasons. First, the Philadelphians did not want the commerce of Baltimore to flourish at the expense of Philadelphia. Second, they insisted that all railroads chartered and built within the borders of the Commonwealth of Pennsylvania should be exclusively owned and operated by Pennsylvania businessmen. Undeterred by this denial, the B&S continued to petition the Pennsylvania State Legislature until its request for a charter passed on March 14, 1832. The politicians soon granted a similar charter for the York & Maryland Line (Y&ML) Railroad Company to build a railroad from York south to the state line to connect with the B&S. On May 19, 1835, the Y&ML was organized in Baltimore with Alexander Nisbet elected as president. The fledgling Y&ML suffered from persistent financial difficulties and lack of necessary resources, so Pennsylvania state legislators allowed the B&S to take over the ailing Y&ML's construction and operations.

On June 27, 1838, dignitaries, railroad officials, and special guests signaled that the long-held dream of an interstate railroad between Maryland and Pennsylvania had finally come true by taking the first symbolic trip from Baltimore to York. The first revenue-generating freight train traveled from Baltimore to York on August 23 of that year.

This 1957 image features the Pennsylvania Railroad sign and cast-iron marker indicating the location of the Mason-Dixon Line. Because of a border dispute between Maryland and Pennsylvania, Charles Mason and Jeremiah Dixon were given the task of surveying the line between 1763 and 1767 to settle the dispute. Hence, the line was named after the two surveyors.

This southbound Pennsylvania Railroad passenger train is passing under the Singer Road Bridge a mile south of New Freedom. The bridge, shown here under construction, linked the Ryer and Bailey family farms. The original wooden bridge was replaced by an iron one that was used for many decades before it was extensively refurbished and modernized in 2020. Singer Road links Main and Front Streets in the borough of New Freedom.

Summit Grove was a large campground established after the Civil War in a grove located in the south end of New Freedom alongside the railroad tracks. This location was named Summit by the B&S Railroad in the 1840s due to the steep grade that existed between Parkton, Maryland, and New Freedom, Pennsylvania. In 1887, the railroad built a modest waiting shed for passengers arriving at and leaving the campgrounds. In 1909, the NCR built a more substantial waiting shed, which is at left in the image. At right is the main entrance to the Summit Grove campgrounds.

Northbound train passengers knew when they were approaching New Freedom. The lights in the windows of a small group of houses at right stand opposite the NF interlocking and signal tower that was built in 1896. Installed in the tower was a Saxby-Farmer 14-lever mechanical machine that controlled six signals, four switches, and four facing point locks. It was taken out of service by PRR General Order No. 727, dated September 25, 1924.

The crew of the NCR money train posed for this picture in front of the NF interlocking and signal tower. The money train would make all the station stops along the line from Baltimore City to York, Pennsylvania, while collecting the revenue generated from ticket/freight sales, company receipts, and company communications and also dropping off the employees' payroll.

Between 1838 and 1884, the New Freedom ticket office was located in the local general store. When construction of the Stewartstown Railroad (SRR) was completed on September 10, 1885, the NCR built a fine frame combination passenger and freight station to handle the increased business that the SRR would generate. The New Freedom passenger station is pictured here in 1912.

This 1912 postcard shows the NCR's New Freedom passenger station at left. To the right of that station is the expanded Stewartstown Railroad station platform that was being constructed so passengers could disembark from the train and connect with NCR trains heading south to Baltimore or north to York.

This photograph shows the enclosed waiting shed at New Freedom in 1916. In a joint agreement between the NCR and Stewartstown Railroad (SRR), both companies agreed to share the construction costs for the enclosed waiting shed on the SRR passenger platform. The waiting shed was completed in 1911, but with the decline in passenger traffic being experienced by both railroads, the building was razed in the late 1940s.

The Franklin Street grade crossing, located just north of Main Street, is pictured here in 1912. At right is where the Whistle Stop Bike Shop is today.

The southbound Liberty Limited is shown passing the New Freedom passenger station in 1944. The Pennsylvania Railroad placed the Liberty Limited in service on September 27, 1925, to run from Washington, DC, to Chicago, Illinois, via Baltimore, Harrisburg, and Pittsburgh. The railroad discontinued the Liberty Limited service on October 27, 1957.

This village in Pennsylvania was first known as Railroad (from the 1830s to the 1850s), then as Strasburg (during the Civil War). Railroad completely lost its identity when the NCR retained the name Shrewsbury for the station it purchased in 1871. This 1917 photograph shows the two-story brick structure that was built in 1857 by Simon and Jesse Klinefelter and originally housed a general store, warehouse for local businesses, small railroad ticket office, and community hall.

Above, Shrewsbury stationmaster J.L. Rohrbough (left) is pictured with his two unidentified assistants in front of the station in 1910. Below, Anna Rohrbough, daughter of the stationmaster, has her hand on the station platform sign and is surrounded by her friends in another photograph taken in 1910.

In this 1910 image, Anna Rohrbough is sitting on a station baggage cart while two of her friends are pushing on it. Anna followed in the footsteps of her father, J.L. Rohrbough, by gaining employment with Pennsylvania Railroad shortly after this photograph was taken. She went on to serve the PRR with distinction for 48 years before retiring. In the background is the gristmill that Simon and Jesse Klinefelter erected in 1845.

This is a southward-looking track view of the town of Railroad, Pennsylvania, as it appeared in 1910. At left is the Jackson Hotel, which was built in 1859 by a Mr. Roy; it is still in operation today as a bed and breakfast. At center-left is the F. Helb & Sons Furniture Factory that was built in 1900. It became the Seiling Furniture Company in 1905 and remained in business until 1971. At right is the general store built by Simon and Jesse Klinefelter.

A northbound freight train is shown passing the Shrewsbury (formerly Railroad), Pennsylvania, passenger station around 1900. Behind the station, the one-story building with two smokestacks is the Helb Tannery, built by Frederick Helb. At its peak, the tannery processed 7,000 hides in one year and shipped them via the NCR.

Shown here is a 1916 view of the section toolhouse located on the east side of the tracks just north of Shrewsbury. Each year, the railroad would conduct a contest to determine which section gang had most properly maintained its toolhouse and grounds. Note the water fountain in the foreground that a section gang built to beautify the grounds.

This small frame combination passenger and freight station measured 16 by 54 feet and was built in 1895 at Seitzland, Pennsylvania. Inside were a small waiting room, ticket office, and freight room, as shown in this 1916 photograph.

Seitzland, Pennsylvania, shown around 1908, derived its name from Nicolas Seitz, who purchased a large tract of land near the railroad and built the first mill in the area. At the height of the town's success, it contained four mills, a hotel, a general store, produce retailers, a furniture factory, an undertaker, a coppersmith, a butcher, a cigar-maker, a wagon-builder, a distiller, and a shoemaker all contributing to the town's economic growth.

Here is a general view of Glen Rock, Pennsylvania, in 1910. Glen Rock was originally named Heathcote after founder William Heathcote, who purchased the Simon Koller farm for $3,425 on March 31, 1837. While the Baltimore & Susquehanna Railroad was constructing its roadway through Heathcote's property, the workers encountered a glen filled with rocks and boulders that needed to be removed. This slowed the contractor's progress, and he started to refer to this area as Glen Rock. On August 29, 1859, an application for the incorporation of the town or borough was submitted to the court for consideration. Heathcote agreed that the town should be named after the railroad contractor who unofficially called the area Glen Rock during construction. At right is the Cold Spring Hotel.

The Water Street grade crossing in Glen Rock is pictured here in 1910. At center-left is the Glen Rock passenger and freight station, which was built in 1856 by Emmanuel Sheffer. It housed the railroad ticket office, a general store, a large meeting room, and the local Glen Rock newspaper and bank. The NCR purchased the station in 1874 and converted it into a combination passenger and freight station. On December 20, 1961, the station was demolished by Mike McMillan, at a cost of $17,000, to make way for a modern gas station.

This 1908 view shows the GR interlocking and signal tower located at the Water Street grade crossing in Glen Rock opposite the passenger station grounds. It was built in 1898 and controlled two signals, a pair of grade crossing gates, two derails, and a crossover. The tower was closed by PRR General Order No. 1306, dated April 9, 1931.

This 25,000-gallon frost-proof water tank in Glen Rock was located on the east side of the tracks just north of the Glen Rock passenger station. The water tank, shown here in 1916, was rebuilt in 1872 by the NCR. Steam engines would often stop at this location to take on water before proceeding.

This 1910 image features a snowy northward-looking view of the main line tracks as seen from the Glen Rock station platform. At left, the southbound signal is in a stop position. Next to the signal is the standpipe where the steam engine would stop and take on water.

This 1920 image shows a southbound passenger train passing the GR Tower (left) and the passenger station (right). In the center behind the steam engine is Simon Koller's sawmill, which was built in 1832. In 1837, William Heathcote, the founder of Glen Rock, purchased the abandoned sawmill, razed it, and built a brick woolen mill on the original foundation. The Heathcote family used the site as a woolen mill until 1852, when they sold it to the firm of Schaeffer and Olp, which immediately converted it into a gristmill. In modern times, the building has been converted into a fine restaurant named the Glen Rock Inn.

This photograph shows the freight station at Larue, which was built in 1913. The 8-by-10-foot frame passenger waiting shelter was constructed in 1906. The small town was surrounded by dairy farms and fruit orchards. A general store, post office, water-powered rolling mill, large icehouse (that could hold up to 200 tons of ice), and local baseball team all contributed to the development of the Larue area.

This view looks south toward coaling facilities around 1910. The coaling facilities were located south of the three-story Hanover Junction Station, which dated to before the Civil War.

A close-up view of the Hanover Junction coaling facilities is shown here in 1916. At left is the pump house, which had the function of assuring that water was pumped to the standpipe. In the center of the photograph is the standpipe, where steam engines would stop to take on water. At right, on the top of the hill, is the wood-frame shanty where the operator of the coaling facilities stayed. The overhead bridge contained chute openings that assured the necessary coal was dropped directly into the engine tender.

This 1916 photograph was taken on the overhead bridge that contained the coal chutes. Note the small coal cars (commonly known as "Larry cars") in the background. They were used to transfer coal from the large coal cars sitting on the high trestle to the west of the main line. Once the Larry cars were loaded, they were pushed by hand into position over the coal chute and then opened. The coal fell through the chute and landed in the tender, where it was stored until it was needed.

Above, a west-facing view of the coaling facilities shows John Henry Heuett, the foreman, in a c. 1910 photograph. Below, the pump house is shown in 1916. It pumped water from the reservoir located on the west side of tracks directly to the standpipes located near the tracks.

This famous Mathew Brady photograph has been reported to have been taken on November 18, 1863, when Pres. Abraham Lincoln traveled through Hanover Junction for the dedication ceremonies of the Soldiers' National Cemetery in Gettysburg. Some observers believe that the tall, stovepipe-hatted man on the platform is Lincoln, and a few Pinkerton guards are standing on top of the freight cars. Many historians have questioned the theory that this is Lincoln and believe that various events that took place at Hanover Junction before the president's trip to Gettysburg prevented him from getting off the train and posing for a photograph.

Passengers on the Western Maryland Railroad took in this westward view of the Hanover Junction Station in 1915. At that time, the first floor featured a kitchen, dining room, living room (for the stationmaster and his family), a passenger waiting room, and an interlocking tower that was being leased by the NCR. On the second floor were four large bedrooms for the stationmaster and his family. The third floor contained 10 small bedrooms that were once part of a hotel that operated within the station.

This northwest-looking view of the Hanover Junction Station was taken by the Pennsylvania Railroad in 1916. This combination hotel and passenger station was built in 1852 by the Hanover Branch Railroad. Between 1855 and 1870, the NCR leased the station portion for its main line passengers while establishing a telegraphy school to train its employees about how to send and take messages over the telegraph. A 17-bed hotel filled the top story of the station, while a common passenger waiting room and separate ticket/telegraph office on the main floor served the traveling public.

Wilfred J. Shaffer (pictured) was the last stationmaster at Hanover Junction when the Pennsylvania Railroad closed the doors of the station and ended its 75-year lease on September 30, 1930.

The village of Smyser Station took its name from Jacob Smyser, who, along with his partner John E. Ziegler, built the area's first store and warehouse in 1839. The above photograph shows the station as it appeared around 1900 before it was converted into a full-time store.

The NCR's passenger waiting shed at Glatfelter Station was named after Casper Glattfelder, an immigrant from Switzerland who settled in the area in 1743. His prominent family went on to build a large paper mill, successful insurance business, and other businesses in the tristate area. On September 25, 1958, the Pennsylvania Railroad sold off the toolhouse and nearby property. Posing in the photograph is Phyllis Glattfelder.

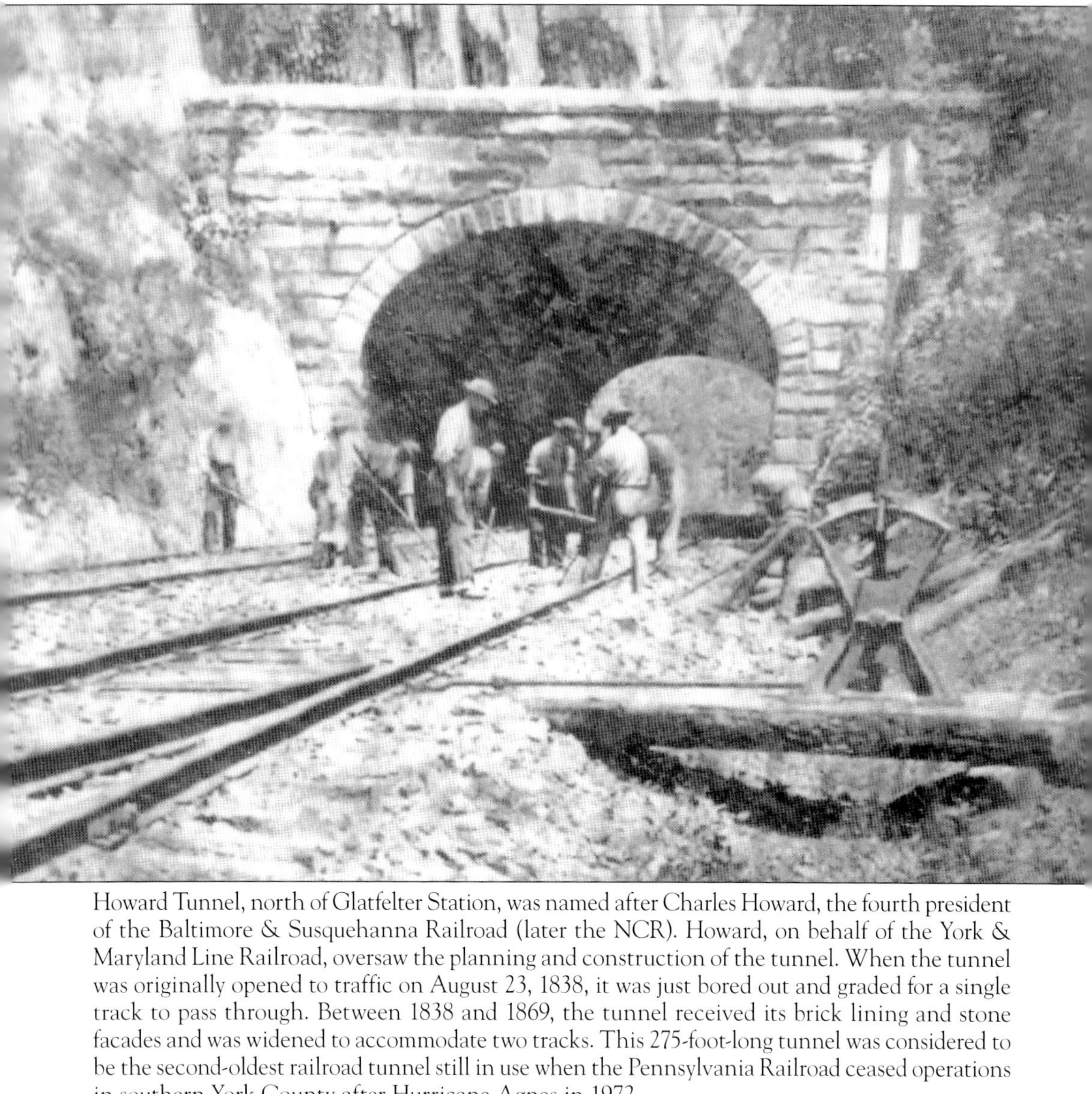

Howard Tunnel, north of Glatfelter Station, was named after Charles Howard, the fourth president of the Baltimore & Susquehanna Railroad (later the NCR). Howard, on behalf of the York & Maryland Line Railroad, oversaw the planning and construction of the tunnel. When the tunnel was originally opened to traffic on August 23, 1838, it was just bored out and graded for a single track to pass through. Between 1838 and 1869, the tunnel received its brick lining and stone facades and was widened to accommodate two tracks. This 275-foot-long tunnel was considered to be the second-oldest railroad tunnel still in use when the Pennsylvania Railroad ceased operations in southern York County after Hurricane Agnes in 1972.

Howard Tunnel was considered to be a choke point for the railroad if it collapsed and or was sabotaged to prevent goods and services from moving up and down the main line. Realizing its importance, the railroad and the US government at times placed employees at the tunnel to report any suspicious activity. During the Civil War and World Wars I and II, the federal government stationed military troops in the area to protect the tunnel. This c. 1940 photograph shows John Senft in front of one of the many temporary watch boxes placed in this location for employees to keep an eye on the tunnel.

In this c. 1920 image, Howard Senft holds the flag at the 8-by-10-foot frame BI interlocking and signal tower at Brillhart. The tower controlled two signals and one crossover that permitted trains to cross from one track to another. The tower was closed by PRR General Order No. 727, dated September 25, 1925.

The village of Brillhart, Pennsylvania, derived its name from Johan Peter Brillhart and his family, who started arriving in the area in the 1730s. This c. 1910 photograph shows the local general store and hotel. The NCR leased a small space within the store for use as a ticket office and waiting room until the late 1930s. A formal passenger station was not built at this location because of the low volume of passenger and freight business.

On Good Friday, April 2, 1920, a southbound Pennsylvania Railroad passenger train derailed at Centerville, a mile north of Glen Rock. The engineman was killed, and three crew members and one passenger were injured. The accident was caused by a broken spring hanger on the lead locomotive. The engineman who died was William H. Dehuff of Baltimore, Maryland. Ironically, Dehuff's son Walter was the superintendent of Read Machinery in Glen Rock and lived close to the scene of the accident. Because it was Good Friday, ridership on this train was low; it usually carried school students between York and Glen Rock.

This image shows Pres. Harry S. Truman's special train used in the 1948 presidential campaign as it was passing Kings Mills Road and heading northward. To the right of the photo is the 8-by-10-foot frame CO (later referred to as Grantley) interlocking and signal tower that was built in 1900 and closed on November 28, 1956. Before the tower closed, it controlled six signals, three switches, two derails, and a set of crossing gates.

This c. 1940s image shows the Grantley Road grade crossing. At right is a watch box.

A watch box located on Main Street in Sunbury, Pennsylvania, is pictured here in 1916. A watchman would come out and lower the gates to prevent the motorist and pedestrian traffic from entering the grade crossing while the train passed. In the background is a hotel called the Hoffman House.

This 1912 postcard view is looking south at the NCR's York passenger station that was built in 1903. This was one of three stations built at this location. The first station was built in 1841, while the second one was constructed in 1863 to accommodate the rapid increase in military business because of the Civil War.

This 1912 postcard view looks north at the NCR's York Station. The passenger station serviced two other connecting railroads in addition to the main line that went from Baltimore, Harrisburg, and Sunbury to Sodus Point, New York. The York Branch Railroad ran eastward from York and crossed over the Susquehanna River to Columbia, Pennsylvania. The second railroad (the York, Hanover & Frederick Branch) ran southwest from York to Hanover and made its final stop in Frederick, Maryland. The station closed its doors to the traveling public on May 1, 1971, when Amtrak ended all passenger service on the main line from Baltimore to Harrisburg.

In 1940, a Mr. Snyder (the engineer at left) and F.B. Rider (the conductor) posed in front of the northbound train they were working on that had stopped in York for service.

In February 1948, Betty J. Lewis took her six-month-old son Bill Lewis to the York Station to watch the trains. Bill sat quietly with his eyes wide open in amazement. These big steam engines, with smoke billowing out of their smokestacks, captured Bill's imagination and interest through the years. That early passion led to Bill becoming a railroad historian, model builder, and collector of railroad memorabilia.

A southbound freight train with engine No. 3833 is shown passing the York Station (right) on April 16, 1946.

This 1915 view looks south toward NCR's freight station buildings in York. The location is Queen Street, with the pedestrian overhead bridge above the railroad tracks. Due to the Queen Street grade crossing being a major road in and out of York, the railroad faced major delays in pedestrian and vehicle traffic. In 1890, the NCR built this pedestrian overhead bridge to reduce the number of fatalities at the grade crossing.

This stairway once led to the pedestrian overhead bridge at the intersection of York and Queen Streets in York. By 1943, because of the reduction in business and pedestrian traffic in the area, the Pennsylvania Railroad razed the overhead bridge.

This southbound freight train, including engine No. 6209, is shown passing the K interlocking and signal tower near the Loucks Mill Road grade crossing on April 17, 1946.

The York Tower was located between Queen Street and Loucks Mill Road. This copper-roofed, two-story brick structure (with a basement) was completed on May 25, 1926. A model No. 14 electropneumatic machine from the Union Switch and Signal Company, with 26 levers, was installed. The machine consisted of 8 levers for 19 signals; 9 levers for 13 switches and 3 derails; 1 lever for 4 electric switch locks; 1 spare space; and 4 spare levers. This photograph was taken around 1940 and shows the York Tower (just right of center).

This 1948 view shows PRR E7A engine No. 5849 and its freight cars heading south past the 12R home signal for the York Tower. Behind the train is the coal wharf where steam engines took on coal. To the right of the coal wharf is a 30,000-gallon water tank where steam engines took on water.

This 1952 photograph looks north and was taken from the signal bridge located near Queen Street. The image shows the engine yard along with the two enginehouses, where service and repair of the engines took place.

This 1940s view shows a southbound freight train passing over the Loucks Mill Road grade crossing. Note the motorcars waiting as the freight train passes. This grade crossing experienced such a high volume of motor traffic that the City of York and the PRR decided to build an overhead bridge, thus eliminating the grade crossing, in the early 1950s.

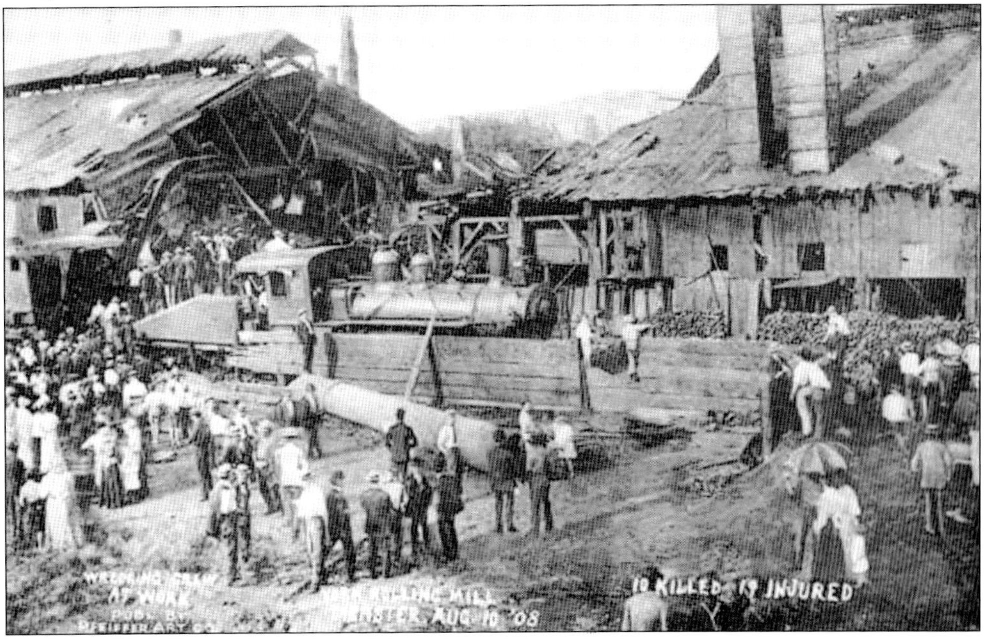

On August 10, 1908, at 2:45 p.m., a poorly maintained boiler in the center of this mill exploded without warning while the employees were going about their duties. The explosion was so loud that it could be heard several miles away. When help arrived, rescuers discovered that the explosion had killed 10 people and injured 19. This mill was founded in 1868, but due to the extensive damage from the explosion, it was forced to close its doors and move its operations elsewhere.

This 1916 northwest-facing view shows NCR Bridge No. 95 at Loucks, which the railroad later redesignated as Bridge No. 58.32. This reinforced concrete slab bridge was rebuilt in 1890 and is still serving the railroad today. Above the bridge (at right) are the 30,000-gallon water tank and pump house where steam engines stopped to take on water before proceeding to their destinations.

The NCR established a station stop at Emig's Grove because of its picturesque views and beautiful groves where one could enjoy a picnic. The railroad built a 12-by-62-foot shelter shed in 1899 to accommodate passengers who wished to stop at or leave from this location. The stop mysteriously disappeared from the schedule in 1901. This c. 1910 photograph shows a southbound freight train getting ready to pass the site where the shelter shed once stood. In the background is the SM interlocking and signal tower that controlled two signals, a crossover, and one switch.

Five

Consolidation

The Commonwealth of Pennsylvania, being progressive as it was, continued to pass legislation to assure its prosperity while protecting Philadelphia and its port. Realizing that canals and railroads would play a big part in the development of the port of Philadelphia, the commonwealth unsuccessfully tried to control the development of railroads within its borders. Since the Baltimore & Susquehanna Railroad (B&S) gained access to Pennsylvania in 1832, competition between the ports of Baltimore and Philadelphia had increased.

To assure economic development and access by railroads in Philadelphia, Pennsylvania legislators granted a charter to the Wrightsville & Gettysburg Railroad (W&G) on February 28, 1837. The company planned to build a line from Gettysburg to York and then from York to Wrightsville, crossing the Susquehanna River there and then connecting to railroads in Columbia that headed to either Harrisburg or to Philadelphia. The W&G borrowed a considerable sum of money from the B&S to construct this railroad. In the meantime, politicians gave perpetual use of the W&G to the York & Maryland Line (Y&ML) Railroad, which the B&S had taken control of in 1838. Because the W&G lacked the funds to purchase railroad equipment, the B&S stepped in as an agent and took control of the railroad. This gave the B&S greater access to Pennsylvania; quietly, the B&S's dream of heading toward York Haven, Pennsylvania, was playing out.

On April 21, 1846, a charter was granted to the York & Cumberland (Y&C) Railroad to construct a railroad from York to Bridgeport (now Lemoyne). When the public stock for the Y&C came up for sale, the B&S purchased enough stock to gain a controlling interest. Not wanting to stop there, the B&S planned to head northward to the coalfields of north-central Pennsylvania. That opportunity materialized when Pennsylvania state legislators granted a charter to the Susquehanna Railroad (SRR) on April 14, 1851, to build a railroad from Bridgeport to Sunbury. Lacking the necessary capital to construct the line, the SRR borrowed a considerable amount of money from the B&S, the Y&ML, and the W&G. The Baltimore & Susquehanna (B&S) Railroad took responsibility for the debts of the SRR by taking control of the railroad. Consolidation occurred on December 16, 1854, when the B&S, the Y&ML, the Y&C, and the SRR merged into one railroad, which was renamed the Northern Central Railway (NCR).

This 1916 photograph shows the front of the train station in Mount Wolf, Pennsylvania. As the Pennsylvania Railroad (PRR) increased its ownership stake and influence within the NCR organization, the NCR began constructing standard combination and freight stations throughout its system that matched the PRR patterns.

The village of Mount Wolf, Pennsylvania, was originally named Mount Campbell after Thomas Campbell, who urged the extension of the Baltimore & Susquehanna (B&S) Railroad to Harrisburg. In the 1850s, the village's name was changed to honor George H. Wolf, whom the B&S had appointed as the stationmaster in 1852. Wolf was also the postmaster and the owner of a local store and warehouse. This c. 1910 image looks northwest at the Mount Wolf tracks and combination passenger and freight station. Behind the station and to the left is the Mount Wolf Furniture Factory.

The Hartman's Road grade crossing is shown in this c. 1930s image. There were five grade crossings in Mount Wolf at the time.

Wago was a junction point where the Atglen and Susquehanna Branch connected with the NCR in 1907. This exclusive low-grade freight line was built to avoid congestion in Philadelphia and Lancaster on the way to Enola. This photograph shows a northward view of the Wago passenger waiting shelter built in 1906; it was removed in the late 1930s. As of 1945, the Baltimore Division of the NCR ended and the Philadelphia Division began at this station.

York Haven, Pennsylvania, took its name from being a haven for transportation down the Susquehanna River. The riverfront canal also played an essential role in the development of York Haven, but the NCR accelerated its development into a regional center of trade and commerce. Leading citizens, realizing the importance of the railroad, encouraged a group of Baltimore businessmen to build a new railroad from Baltimore to York Haven. This 1910 photograph, featuring a southeast-facing view, shows the combination passenger and freight station that the railroad erected in 1887.

This 1912 postcard view looks south toward York Haven. Note the two tracks at left; they belonged exclusively to the low-grade freight line of the Atglen and Susquehanna Branch.

The image on this c. 1930 postcard faces southwest toward the Susquehanna River and shows the York Haven passenger station. Note the considerable buildup of ice that was typical along the river in the cold winter months. On occasions, large chunks of ice spilled over the embankment onto the railroad tracks and obstructed the movement of trains until crews cleared it.

This northward view features the MR interlocking and signal tower (later known as Cly Tower) as it appeared around 1910. This 16-by-38-foot two-story brick structure with a basement was completed in 1906. It contained an Armstrong machine that featured 40 mechanical levers to control the switches and signals for the movement of passenger and freight trains along the main line of the NCR. On June 29, 1983, by General Order No. 2-191, the Consolidated Rail Corporation (Conrail) closed the tower, and Conrail subsequently demolished it on November 6, 1986.

Once known as Falls, this area's name was changed to Cly to honor Cly Shelly, a young and ambitious merchant who helped to kick-start the town's economic growth. Above is a postcard view of Cly showing the combination passenger and freight station built in 1894 and the Falls (later renamed Cly) interlocking and signal tower constructed in 1906.

Cly Shelly was responsible for encouraging the America Phosphorus Mills, which produced matches, to locate in the town next to the main line of the NCR in 1906. The mill and its sidings are pictured here in 1910.

This is a 1940s postcard showing the ruins of the Charles Felt and Paper Company in Cly. The structure was built in 1903. William L. Miller, a local resident and master carpenter, supervised the construction of the mill. Behind the ruins are the old American Phosphorus Mills.

This 1910 postcard shows a northward view of the tracks with the Goldsboro, Pennsylvania, passenger station at left. At right are the two tracks belonging to the Atglen and Susquehanna Branch, which was built in 1907. This was a low-grade freight line that was created to avoid congestion in Philadelphia so trains could easily gain access to the Enola freight yard just north of West Fairview Station.

Goldsboro, Pennsylvania, was originally known as Hussey's Ferry because of a nearby ferry service that businessman Nathan Hussey established to cross the Susquehanna River in 1743. On August 23, 1864, when the borough was incorporated, the name was changed to Goldsboro to honor distinguished civil engineer J.M. Goldsborough of the York & Cumberland Railroad. This 1915 photograph shows the typical Pennsylvania Railroad standard combination passenger and freight station; this one was built in Goldsboro in 1874 and demolished in 1960.

Middletown Ferry derived its name from being the halfway point between Lancaster and Carlisle. It was the western terminus for the Union Canal Company, which the Commonwealth of Pennsylvania authorized to construct a canal from Philadelphia to Pittsburgh. When the York & Cumberland Railroad (later the NCR) was completed on February 10, 1851, Middletown Ferry became a transportation hub for a canal, ferry, and railroad, which led to its economic development. The NCR passenger waiting shelter is pictured here in 1916.

River View, Pennsylvania, derives its name from the scenic vista overlooking the Susquehanna River. A nearby hotel and general store served as a getaway spot for residents of Baltimore, York, and Harrisburg who wanted to escape the heat of summer in the city. This is a 1915 view of the passenger waiting shelter.

Marsh Run got its name from many marshes located in the general area. A hotel served as the railroad station until 1876, when the NCR built the first passenger waiting shed. Because of the harsh winters, the NCR rebuilt the passenger waiting shelter and enclosed it, as shown in this 1916 photograph.

This 1910 postcard view looks south into New Cumberland, Pennsylvania. The tracks at far left are the low-grade freight tracks belonging to the Atglen and Susquehanna Branch. At right is the New Cumberland combination passenger and freight station that was built in 1886. Behind the station is the Pennsylvania Dye and Bleach Works.

New Cumberland, formerly known as Haldermanstown, has its name changed in August 1827 in order to avoid postal confusion with Cumberland, Maryland. This 1916 photograph shows the Pennsylvania Railroad's standard design for combination passenger and freight stations.

Lemoyne, Pennsylvania, was known as Bridgeport in the 19th century. A junction was created at this location when the York & Cumberland Railroad (later the NCR) crossed the main line of the Cumberland Valley (CV) Railroad on February 10, 1851, to connect with the Susquehanna Railroad (also later absorbed into the NCR) that ran north to Sunbury, Pennsylvania. This 1916 northward-facing view shows the Philadelphia, Harrisburg & Pittsburgh Railroad's overhead bridge, which was built in 1890 to connect Harrisburg with Lurgan in Franklin County. At both left and right are station platforms for the NCR.

This is Lemoyne as it appeared in 1900. This is a general view of the CV Railroad and its yard tracks. The passenger station at left was built in 1893. At center are the J tower and the main line of the NCR.

The J interlocking and signal tower, shown here in 1890, was situated between the crossing of the Cumberland Valley (CV) Railroad and the NCR. The tower was built in 1885 with Armstrong levers that were mechanically attached to the signal and switches. On March 13, 1907, the NCR and CV updated and modernized the J tower by installing a Union Switch and Signal Company model No. 14 electropneumatic machine. In the early 1930s, the tower's name was changed to LEMO. It continued to control the movement of traffic between the two railroads until the early 1980s, when Conrail removed the tower from service. In the late 1980s, the tower was disassembled; it was then reassembled in Strasburg, Pennsylvania.

This 1908 view of Rockville, Pennsylvania, shows the bridge that connected the railroad from Pittsburgh to Harrisburg and Philadelphia. The first single-track bridge was a wooden covered bridge that was completed in August 1849. It was 3,681 feet long with 23 Howe truss spans reinforced by Burr trusses on the outside of the bridge. As business increased, the wooden bridge began to show wear and tear. Also, Pennsylvania Railroad officials feared that sparks from steam engines crossing the old bridge could set it on fire. In 1877, the company decided to replace the covered bridge with a two-track iron deck that utilized the existing stone piers of the first bridge. At center is the third bridge, which was built in 1902. At the time, it was considered to be the longest stone-arch bridge in the world. The piers of the original bridge are visible at left.

The rare night view on this c. 1910 postcard features the third bridge built at Rockville. The second bridge proved to be inadequate and was restricting the profitability of the Pennsylvania Railroad's main line from Philadelphia to Pittsburgh. Therefore, company officers decided to build a four-track stone-arch bridge across the Susquehanna River downstream from the existing two-track iron truss bridge. In 1900, 800 workers started constructing 48 stone arches spanning 3,802 feet. Each stone arch is 52 feet high and measures 70 feet across. The bridge had a price tag of $975,150 and required 220,000 tons of stone and an estimated 600,000 barrels of cement. On March 30, 1902, the bridge was completed and opened to railroad traffic.

Pictured in 1912 is the RJ (Rockville) interlocking and signal tower, which was built in 1898. This tower originally had Armstrong levers that were mechanically attached to the switches and signals. In 1942, the tower was updated, and a Union Switch and Signal Company model No. 14 electropneumatic machine was installed to control 38 signals and 40 switches. In 1986, the Consolidated Rail Corporation (Conrail) closed the tower as part of cost-cutting measures. The tracks behind the tower were the NCR's main line.

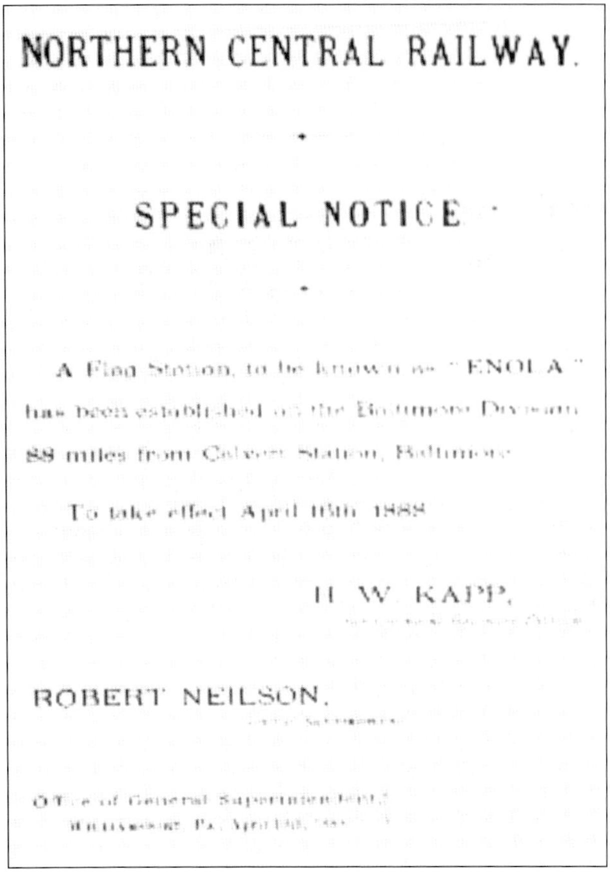

NORTHERN CENTRAL RAILWAY.

SPECIAL NOTICE

A Flag Station, to be known as "ENOLA" has been established on the Baltimore Division 88 miles from Calvert Station, Baltimore.

To take effect April 18th 188[illegible]

H. W. KAPP,

ROBERT NEILSON,

Office of General Superintendent,
Williamsport, Pa., April [illegible]

On April 18, 1884, the NCR issued a special notice to establish a flag stop named Enola to honor the daughter of the farmer who sold the property to its parent company, the Pennsylvania Railroad. In exchange for the sale of the property, the farmer requested that a station stop be established and named after his only daughter.

This 1901 image shows the start of the excavation and grading of the Enola classification and freight yard. By the end of 1903, more than 3,000 men were involved in its construction. The project cost $7 million. In January 1905, the Enola yard opened.

This is a 1917 view looking north at the NCR's main line tracks at Enola. The overhead bridge is a local trolley crossing. On the other side of the overhead bridge, and visible underneath it, is the DY interlocking and signal tower. This tower controlled the movements of trains on the NCR's main line and those entering and exiting the Enola classification and freight yard.

The Enola classification and freight yard is shown in 1916. When the yard was fully completed in the late 1920s, it encompassed 316 acres and had the capacity to store 9,692 freight cars. It was the largest freight yard in the world at the time.

This is a 1916 view of the Enola combination freight and passenger station on the main line of the NCR, opposite the Enola classification and freight yard.

The 43-stall circular roundhouse and nearby turntable, which were used to service and store steam engines at the Enola classification and freight yard, are pictured in this 1916 image.

The Pennsylvania Railroad built a baseball field and grandstands, shown here in 1916, in Enola to encourage its employees to remain healthy, strong, and active. The railroad encouraged all of its divisions to sponsor baseball teams for a yearly company-wide tournament. The PRR supported several other organized sports activities in addition to baseball.

Marysville, Pennsylvania, was known as Haley until 1867, when the Commonwealth of Pennsylvania granted a reincorporation of the borough, and the name was changed. The borough became a hub for passenger and freight trains when the first passenger station and freight yard were built here in 1859. The second station, shown on this 1912 postcard, was built in 1900. In the mid-1950s, the Pennsylvania Railroad closed this station to the traveling public and ended all local passenger service.

Above is an 1890 view of the train dispatcher's office, yardmaster's office, and the interlocking and signal tower that controlled all of the movements of the trains within the classification and freight yard in Marysville.

This is a 1912 postcard view of the Marysville classification and freight yard. The yard was about halfway between Baltimore and Canandaigua, New York, and provided storage for idle freight cars and engines that were waiting to be classified to head for top point while avoiding any further congestion that might be experienced in Harrisburg, Philadelphia, York, or elsewhere.

The 36-stall circular stone roundhouse and turntable used to service and shelter steam engines at the Marysville classification and freight yard is shown here in the 1870s.

A section track gang poses in front of their Marysville shanty in this 1870s image. Note the roundhouse at left. This track gang was assigned to maintain and service all switches and track structures within the limits of the Marysville classification and freight yard.

This 1912 postcard view of the NCR's main line looks south at Dauphin, Pennsylvania. In the distance is where the NCR built the Dauphin Bridge to span the Susquehanna River in 1858. This bridge allowed the NCR to cross from the west bank of the river to the east side to head northward, passing Dauphin and proceeding toward Sunbury. The first train crossed the bridge on April 5, 1858.

Dauphin was known as Fort Lyon until the borough was incorporated in 1845, and the name was changed. This 1916 image shows the NCR's main line tracks at left and the old Dauphin & Susquehanna (D&S) Railroad tracks at right. The D&S made its connection with the NCR main line in Dauphin in 1854. The Philadelphia & Reading Railroad took over the D&S Railroad in 1872. The route was abandoned in 1939 after a fire destroyed the bridge outside of Pine Grove.

Speeceville, Pennsylvania, was named after Lloyd Speece, the founder and first settler in the area; the village is located four miles northwest of Dauphin at the foot of Peter's Mountain. A nearby iron furnace, sawmill, canal, and the NCR encouraged the growth of Speeceville. The small frame freight station and flag stop where tickets could be purchased is shown here in 1916.

Clark's Ferry, Pennsylvania, was named after Daniel Clark, who established the first ferry to cross the Susquehanna River from the west side to the east in 1788. In 1790, Clark built a tavern to accommodate travelers journeying across the river. When the Commonwealth of Pennsylvania completed a wooden 2,088-foot-long covered bridge in 1829, Clark's ferry business suffered and eventually closed. When the Susquehanna Railroad (later part of the main line of NCR) was completed in 1856, the tracks and station were close enough to the canal that boats could stop at Clark's Ferry and unload passengers and goods so they could travel by rail to destinations that the canal system did not service. This 1917 photograph looks northwest toward the combination freight and passenger station that was rebuilt in 1878.

This is how the Clark's Ferry stationmaster's house appeared in 1916. The house was located just north of the station. The railroad provided its stationmasters with living quarters if the station location was in a remote area where it would be difficult to commute or housing was nonexistent. In later years, this building became a bunkhouse for railroad employees who needed to remain in the area due to the weather, track conditions, or a train wreck.

"Inglenook" means "the space on either side of the fireplace." Therefore, the name Inglenook was given to this summer resort and community because it was situated in the middle of a route between two major cities—Philadelphia and Pittsburgh. Many summer cottages were built to allow vacationers to take advantage of the scenery, clean air, and easy accessibility to the railroad. This 1916 photograph shows the passenger waiting shelter that was erected in 1892.

Halifax, Pennsylvania, was originally known as Fort Halifax due to it being a temporary stronghold for the Pennsylvania colonial militia during the French and Indian War from 1756 to 1757. The Susquehannock tribe had lived in the area until Europeans started arriving, forcing indigenous peoples to relocate. On May 29, 1785, the Commonwealth of Pennsylvania incorporated the borough of Halifax. To continue the town's development, the commonwealth built a canal from Clark's Ferry to Millersburg to assist in the movement of passengers and goods. The discovery of coal in the region, coupled with the construction of the Susquehanna Railroad (later part of the NCR) in 1856, allowed for further opportunities for growth in Halifax. This 1917 photograph shows the Halifax combined passenger and freight station, which was rebuilt in 1884 at the intersection where Armstrong Street crosses the tracks.

This 1916 view looks south and shows the railroad facilities and tracks in the borough of Halifax. At left, in front of the station, stands the UR interlocking and signal tower that controlled two switches, one derail, and two signals.

Daniel Miller founded the town of Millersburg, Pennsylvania, in 1807. The original passenger station was built just south of Millersburg at the junction where the Lykens Valley Railroad connected with the NCR in 1856. In 1896, the NCR built a stone Queen Anne–style passenger station at Center Street and West Alley. It served the traveling public until 1960, when the railroad shut down the facility. In 1982, the Millersburg Historical Society acquired the station and restored it. The above image offers a view looking northeast toward the passenger station in 1916. The 1916 photograph below, also taken in Millersburg, shows the combination freight office and baggage station located just south of the passenger station.

This 1917 photograph shows the freight and transfer station located just north of the Millersburg passenger station. The freight yard handled inbound and outbound freight and coal trains coming from Sunbury or proceeding off the Lykens Valley Railroad. Helper engines stood by in the yard to assist any coal trains that needed extra power.

Two 35,000-gallon, frost-proof water tanks were located just north of the Millersburg freight and transfer station. On average, depending on the type of steam engine and the type of service, a tender could hold between 1,500 and 2,000 gallons of water.

This dam was built by the NCR to supply water to the two 35,000-gallon water tanks located in the freight yard just north of Millersburg. The railroad would dam a stream, then a pipe would be run from the dam to a nearby pumping station to pump water directly into the tanks.

This section track crew is shown maintaining the track structure just south of Millersburg in 1910. The crew is checking for loose spikes and measuring the gauge between the rails.

John Staily and his family, who were immigrants from Liverpool, England, arrived in this area in 1808 and dubbed it Liverpool after their former hometown. On May 4, 1832, the Commonwealth of Pennsylvania incorporated the borough of Liverpool. The 1914 photograph shows a southward-facing front view of the combination freight and passenger station located on the east bank of the Susquehanna River next to the canal.

This is a 1914 view looking north toward the backside of the Liverpool passenger station. The stationmaster and his family lived on the second floor. Note the balcony that provided a scenic view of the railroad and the Susquehanna River.

The Liverpool canal freight station is shown above in 1914. The crane in front of the station would swing over to the canal, and the operator would lower ropes to lift freight out of the canal boats that was to be shipped by rail.

At left is a 1914 view of the back of the canal freight station at Liverpool. Canal boats would pull up alongside the freight station and unload goods that were designated to be shipped by rail. Not shown in the photograph is a set of steps that allowed passengers on the canal boats to disembark and walk to the railroad station.

Mahantango Valley, Pennsylvania, derives its name from a Delaware (Lenape) word meaning "we had plenty to eat." This 1916 image shows the small passenger station at left and a large residence that the railroad owned and rented out.

The railroad had various sections to assure proper maintenance and upkeep. Each section was assigned a track foreman and four to six trackmen. Each day, the track gang would walk its assigned section to maintain the tracks and any railroad structures within that section. Railroad officials encouraged friendly competition among the sections to inspire pride and creativity. Each year, the railroad company held a contest. The track gang that maintained its section to the high standards expected by the railroad would be awarded a prize. This 1916 picture features a watch box that a track gang designed and built at Dalmatia, Pennsylvania.

Dalmatia, Pennsylvania, was originally known as Georgetown after George Brosius founded it in 1798. Sometime between 1898 and 1916, the railroad changed the station's name to Dalmatia because of the large population of Croatians living in the region. Pictured here in 1917 is the combination passenger and freight station that was built in 1886.

Herndon, Pennsylvania, was originally known as Trevorton Junction because of the Trevorton & Susquehanna Railroad (later renamed the Trevorton, Mahanoy & Susquehanna Railroad). In 1855, the company erected a bridge across the Susquehanna River to connect Port Trevorton with the NCR on the east bank of the river. The Trevorton & Susquehanna Railroad continued constructing the line until it reached Shamokin to increase coal shipments in the region. This 1917 photograph shows the frame 19-by-54-foot combination passenger and freight station that was built in 1885.

The bunkhouse at Herndon is shown in this 1915 image. The 16-by-20-foot two-story frame structure provided a place where the yard crews and crews that handled coal and freight trains could rest between shifts before making their return trips.

Steam engines of the era required a significant amount of water, so the NCR built two 35,000-gallon, frost-proof water tanks at Herndon to meet the demands of its railroad as well as those of the Trevorton & Susquehanna Railroad. The water tanks are featured in this 1917 image.

Capt. Anthony Selin, who fought with George Washington during the Revolutionary War, founded the town of Selinsgrove, Pennsylvania, in 1787. Selinsgrove became a junction when the Sunbury & Lewistown Railroad connected with the NCR in December 1871. Immediately after completion of the line, the Pennsylvania Railroad leased it. The 1916 photograph above shows the 32-by-32-foot three-story NCR passenger station that was built in 1861 and demolished in 1932.

With the outbreak of World War I, the federal government feared that German spies or sympathizers for the German cause who lived in the United States would sabotage railroad bridges and tunnels. Because of this fear, the military posted guards at strategic bridges and tunnels in order to prevent any planned sabotage. This 1917 photograph shows a military guard posted next to the Selinsgrove Bridge, which spanned the Susquehanna River and allowed trains on the Sunbury & Lewistown Railroad to enter Sunbury or go south to Harrisburg.

This 1910 postcard view shows the NCR tracks as they narrow before entering the town of Sunbury. The NCR route through this region was known for its charm and scenic beauty.

Sunbury, Pennsylvania, was known as Shamokin when it was founded in 1727. When the Commonwealth of Pennsylvania granted the borough's incorporation in 1772, the name was changed to Sunbury after a town located in Spelthorne, England. This is a 1910 postcard view of the Sunbury (Pennsylvania) passenger station that was completed on June 1, 1872, at a cost of $35,000. On the first floor were men's and women's waiting rooms, a telegraph office, a baggage room, and a mail and express room. The second floor had general office space that was rented to other railroads operating in Sunbury. The station still stands today and is a reminder of the glorious past of the Northern Central Railway and the Pennsylvania Railroad.

In this 1917 photograph, a crowd of well-wishers gathered to greet and wave to the men and women who answered Uncle Sam's call to serve in the armed forces to protect freedom abroad. Many servicemen and women on the train were from Sunbury.

The Sunbury freight office, shown here in 1916, was located north of Sunbury near a large freight yard that accommodated all trains that converged on the town.

This 1917 image shows the NCR's frame 16-by-136-foot freight and transfer station at Sunbury, which was built in 1890 north of the city. It provided services for the Shamokin Valley & Pottstown Railroad, which opened in 1834; the Sunbury & Erie Railroad, which started operations in 1855; and the Susquehanna Railroad, which began in 1858.

Pictured in 1916 is one of the first all-steel, 70,000-gallon, frost-proof water tanks built along the route of the Northern Central Railway at Sunbury. It provided water for the steam engines and freight railroad facilities in the area. Below the tank is the section toolhouse.

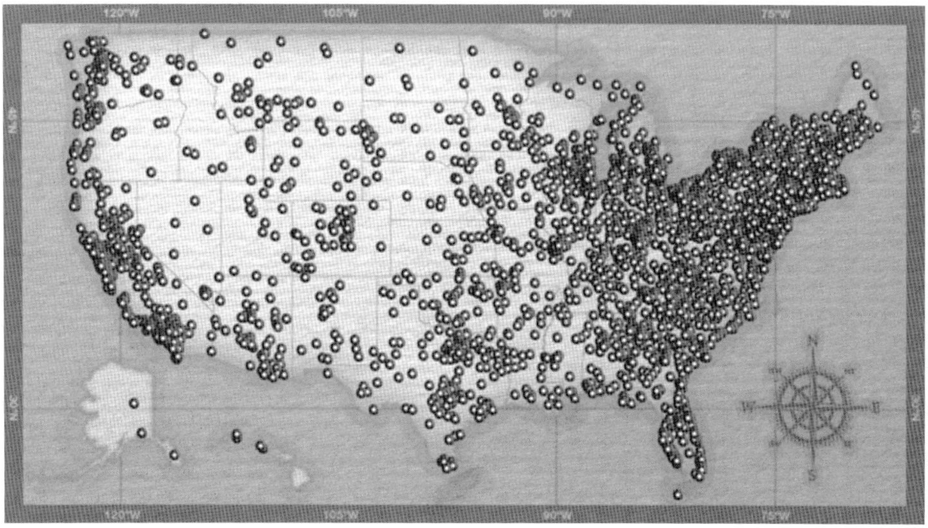